What Peopl

"If you want to see what living out the Great Commission looks like today, read Victor's book. His fascinating stories will stir your heart, thrill your soul and speak Jesus into your life as it did mine. Glory!"

Wayne Atcheson – *Historian of the Billy Graham Library*

"'*As You Go'* will inspire and encourage you about serving God. Victor shares remarkable stories showing us how to be living proof of the PURPOSE of our lives, which is to plant seeds about Jesus '*As We Go*' through daily life. It is a MUST read! It will transform your life!

Mark Whitacre – *The Informant (2009) played by Matt Damon, former executive at ADM, COO at CBMC (Christian Business Men's Connection)*

"A Must Read! This book is Victor's testimony of how God changes the world one person at a time. He has been faithful to do his part, sharing Christ with anyone who will listen, all in the context of his life as a businessman. This book shows that it is not just the preacher on Sunday morning who is gifted to share the Good News."

Tim Philpot – *Kentucky State Senator, Family Court Judge, Former President of CBMC International, author and speaker*

"Using his wonderful gift for telling the stories of his life as practical illustrations, Victor energizes those stories with his passion for sharing the Good News of Jesus Christ. The result is both a great read and a powerful tool that equips and encourages you and me to step into our own stories with the life-giving intention of always being prepared to share Jesus, '*As You Go.*'"

Doug Hunter – *Former CEO, Fellowship of Companies for Christ International (FCCI), Leader in the Global Marketplace Movement*

Spark a Conversation that Impacts Eternity!

Victor Dawson

Cover Design by: Scott Rasmussen
Edited by: Mark Miller
Interior Design by: Loraina Wang, Westerly Creative Studio

For Worldwide Distribution. Printed in the United States of America

ISBN: 978-1-7331253-1-4

Many thanks to Nan, my beautiful and faithful wife and companion for 45 years, and to Jesus for giving me the stories in my life and guiding me in the writing of this book and the As You Go ministry.

Be Blessed, As You Go!

Victor Dawson

Acknowledgements

Special thanks to Chuck Williams, Marty Campfield, Mike Langdon, and Mark Whitacre for their help and encouragement during the writing of this book. Their comments and suggestions helped greatly.

Also, thanks to Patrick O'Neal, Enrique Cepeda, Paul Johnson, Craig Smith, Del Tackett, Dennis Scruggs, Bill Wilking, Bill McAvinney, Chad Hovind, Sean McDowell, Phil Stone, Jim Petersen, Charlynne Boddie, Jim Sigler, Karl Bruce, Mark Hofert, Phil Maginelli, Dave Rathkamp, Holly McAfee, Ross Hill, Dave Balinski, Ted Woodrow, Jimmy Kwong, Doug Hunter, Phil Baggerly, Dick Ellis, Tim Philpot, Wayne Atcheson, Mark Batterson, Dr. Darryl Bock, and Benny Yang.

A Very Special Thanks to:

CBMC USA and CBMC International
Christian Business Men's Connection

I am especially grateful to this wonderful organization for having a huge impact in my life. It started about halfway through my career when one of the managers I worked with, Chuck Williams, invited me to the weekly men's group. Then I was discipled using Operation Timothy by an attorney, Dick Ellis, in Houston for two years. We moved to Denver and I participated locally and started doing life-on-life discipleship. Along the way, I discovered that my purpose in life was Evangelism and Discipleship, the mission of CBMC.

CBMC was founded in 1930 in Chicago and has spread across the U.S. and to almost 100 countries around the world with the message of the Gospel.

This book has many references to CBMC — the people, the stories, the tools and the programs. I can't share what God is doing in my life and why I believe He wanted me to write this book without including a lot about CBMC. Many thanks and blessings to all the faithful, past and present, in this great organization who are having eternal impact, **As They Go**.

What to Expect

This book is filled with stories from ordinary people like me who are living out Jesus' command in Matthew 28:19 "to make disciples of all nations," ***As You Go***. The purpose for writing this book is to ignite, instruct, and inspire all Christians to live out the Great Commission, as they go along their way every day and everywhere with family, friends, neighbors, co-workers, and strangers — resulting in a powerful movement in the Body of Christ in the U.S. and worldwide.

God gave me an unimaginable vision about how he might use me to be part of a new Great Revival or Awakening in His Kingdom on earth on February 19, 2012. I was flying from Chicago to Beijing and had been reading a wonderful book about big dreams from Mark Batterson called *The Circle Maker*. After dinner on this long flight, I settled in to start reading this book again.

And for the first time in my life, God spoke almost audibly to me through the Holy Spirit. He said, "Put down the book, get out a piece of paper, and draw some circles. My first thought was that I didn't know how to draw the circles because I had not finished reading the book. But God repeated His instructions to me, so I got out a notepad and drew circles of God-sized dreams in my life led by the Holy Spirit. It was an incredible experience!

I drew eight circles that day on the plane as I sat quietly praying and listening to the Lord. Some of the first circles were about personal relationships, my lifetime purpose, finances, and giving. Circle # 6 was the most difficult to comprehend. The big dream for this circle was that the adventure God had me on to live out the Great Commission and convince others to do the same would eventually lead to ***one million decisions for Christ! Wow!***

It would take another 18 months after I drew that circle to even have a clue about how that would happen. Then God spoke to me for the second time in my life. That story is in Chapter 2. And yet, I still don't quite know how to wrap my head around this.

As you begin reading this book, I'll first share the reality in our culture now and discuss why so few Christians are telling others about Jesus.

Then I will give you some simple but impactful advice about the ways and steps for you to become an effective Ambassador for Christ — what it would look like if you choose to obey the Great Commission. Who would you become? What would you do? How would you equip yourself for this wonderful life experience?

And finally, I will explain the relationship between evangelism and discipleship and discuss the importance of making disciples and spiritual reproduction.

Throughout the book there are many wonderful real-life stories that have happened to me and others as we did our best to live out the Great Commission, ***As We Go***.

My hope and prayer is that you will be excited to join a multitude of ***As You Go Ambassadors*** and get inspired and engaged to live out the Great Commission.

Let's get started. I truly hope you enjoy the journey, ***As You Go***.

Victor Dawson

Contents

Introduction 1

Part 1 - Jesus Said "Go" 9

Chapter 1 – Facts Tell the Story! 16

Chapter 2 – God Told Me To! 21

Chapter 3 – Are You in Full-Time Ministry? 40

Chapter 4 – Two Great Commands from Jesus! 52

Chapter 5 – Why Don't More Believers Share? 63

Part 2 - What Does "As You Go" Look Like? 75

Chapter 6 - Always Pray First 77

Chapter 7 – Use Words Only if Necessary 89

Chapter 8 – Let God Transform You 98

Chapter 9 – Be Alert and Available at All Times 105

Chapter 10 – As You Go, Make Disciples! 117

Chapter 11 – Relationships Matter! 126

Chapter 12 – Gentleness and Respect! 136

Chapter 13 – Stories Are Interesting, Yours and Mine 146

Chapter 14 – Invitations May Be All You Need! 156

Chapter 15 – Stay in Touch and Keep Praying! 166

Part 3 - Changing Lives, One at a Time! 177

Chapter 16 – Making Your Life Count! 181

Chapter 17 – Reaching the Unconvinced! 189

Chapter 18 – Discipling All Nations 200

Chapter 19 – Operation Timothy 207

Final Thoughts 225

Notes & References

Additional Resources

AsYouGo Website

As You Go 2.0

Introduction

As I was sitting at Gate 21 in the San Diego International Airport very early one morning, I looked through the glass wall at the United Airlines plane that would hopefully take me home to Denver. My wife, Nan, and I had been visiting my aunt in Carlsbad for a couple of weeks, and I needed to get back before she did for some meetings. I was on the standby list for the flight, so my thoughts were a little anxious as I wondered if I would get a seat.

I had just taken out my daily devotional book and my journal and started to spend a short "quiet" time reading and praying.

Suddenly, a booming noise erupted from about 20 feet behind me at the gate. Given the state of our world today, my first thought was of a gunshot or some type of explosion. But the noise did not sound like either. It sounded like someone had dropped a bowling ball on the floor from about six feet high. The sound was so loud that it shook me up a bit.

I quickly turned around to look in the direction of the unexpected noise behind me. As I stood up to see the situation better, I noticed a woman lying face down on the floor. She was probably in her late 40s or early 50s, and I had briefly noticed her sitting there reading a book when I first arrived at the gate.

So, what had happened? I feared it was not good — horrible, actually. And I was right. Apparently, as eyewitnesses sitting near her told me, she started having a massive seizure, but it was unclear whether it was due to a heart attack or a stroke. In severe pain, the lady tried to stand up from her seat, and as she did, she fell straight over with her face and head hitting the carpeted concrete floor with a forceful thud. It was not a bowling ball hitting the floor — it was her head.

Several people nearby came to her aid, and someone yelled to call 911. A doctor was in the gate area and he pushed his way through the crowd of people to get to the lady. He immediately rolled her over on her back, checked for signs of a pulse and breathing, and then started CPR. She was not responding, and things were not looking good from what I could see.

You know how when something like this or an accident happens to you or around you, it seems like it either happened in a flash or that it takes an eternity? For me that morning, it was as if everything was in slow motion. I could imagine this lady in pain, trying to stand up and then falling forward and slamming her face into the carpet-covered concrete floor. But there was nothing going on in slow motion as I heard this loud thud when she landed. The sound still haunts me now, even after several years.

But let's get back to the story: It seemed to me like the paramedics and emergency personnel were taking forever to arrive on the scene. Various people continued to give her CPR without interruption — but to no avail. Finally, emergency vehicles pulled up right by the plane outside of our gate and made their way up the steps to the concourse. In retrospect, probably only 10 to 12 minutes transpired from the time of the call to their arrival, but it really seemed like a long time.

The paramedics quickly started an IV and did all the other things you've seen a hundred times on TV. After a couple of minutes, they prepared the stretcher to transport the lady to the hospital. By this time, even from where I was standing about 20 feet away, I could tell that her face was beginning to turn blue.

Why am I beginning this book with such a horrific tragedy? It was a shocking and sobering event for me and for all the people at the gate. First of all, that incident or something just as awful could happen to any of us — at any moment — without warning. The second reason that this incident had such a profound impact on me is that it had only been slightly over a year since I had undergone emergency open-heart surgery. What just happened at Gate 21 could easily have happened to me. But thankfully, my wife was a lioness with my cardiologist to do further testing (after I had shortness of breath running between gates at the LAX airport), but I passed my stress test with flying colors. She told the doctor that she did not care what the results showed, asserting there was something seriously wrong with me, and she had been trying to convince him for over a year that I was not OK.

I was blessed by God to allow my heart problem to be found and corrected before serious damage or a fatal event occurred. This lady, however, was just sitting at the airport, reading a book and planning to fly to Denver in a short time. I don't know if she was going home to Denver, going to see family there, taking a vacation, or transferring to another destination at the Denver airport. Who knows? But one thing is fairly certain: She was not expecting to die that morning. She had plans for the day and for many days in the future. And what if she was flying to see her grandchildren or family in Denver? Can you imagine their reaction to a phone call while waiting at the airport to pick up their loved one — that she would not be coming today, and further, that they would never see her alive again on earth? How do you explain that to young grandchildren?

So many things were running through my mind at the moment, and the truth is that I don't know the outcome. I was praying, and I'm sure many others nearby were also praying. So maybe God spared her life and she made a complete recovery and is again enjoying her time with family and friends. I would not want to wager a cup of coffee on it though (especially one of those $6 fancy lattes at Starbucks).

As this tragic scene was nearing its end, a businessman was just arriving at the gate and walked up next to me. Likely in his late 50s or early 60s, he was carrying a backpack with the IBM logo on it. "What's going on?", the man asked me, while he stretched to see over the crowd.

I briefly explained what had happened. Then he said, "Wow, that's really awful!"

"Yes, it might be really awful," I replied, "but it all depends on what you believe about where you're going when you die. I for one believe that I'll spend eternity in Heaven with Jesus, and so it won't be awful. It will be fantastic when

I die! Do you know where you're going?"

His face showed a bit of surprise at my question, but then he said, "Well, I hope so."

I took that response to mean that he thinks he's a pretty good person and he's done some good things in his life, so he hopes it will be good enough for God to let him through the Pearly Gates. But it's my belief that unless you have accepted the free gift of salvation through the blood of Jesus Christ on the Cross, all the good works in the world are not going to be enough.

As the crowd now started to disperse and the businessman was about to walk away, I said to him, "If you're not certain where you're going when you die, you should give some serious thought to Jesus and His forgiveness of sin." He turned to leave, and I added, "Safe travels. Hope to see you again." He turned his head back and said, "Thanks. Take care."

I want to point out a very basic but important aspect of ***As You Go***. When the man first came up beside me and spoke, I chose to engage him in conversation. I immediately started to pray for God to lead me through this encounter with the right words and attitude. After I briefly explained what had happened and he said how awful it was, I could have just grunted the word "yeah", and that would have been it.

But I sensed that God wanted me to step out in faith, seize this opportunity that He was orchestrating, and engage in conversation. So I boldly said what I did.

Many Christians would be asking me why I didn't tell him the whole story. Why didn't I make sure that he understood that doing some good works was not going to get him to Heaven and that if he didn't repent and accept Jesus that he was going to spend eternity in Hell with the Devil and all the other evil people? Why didn't I even take a gentler approach and at least explain the whole Gospel message to him and try to close the deal? You know: Jesus was born of the Virgin Mary, was crucified, died and was buried, and then was resurrected on the third day.

The main reason I didn't do that is because God didn't tell me to. I had a brief encounter with this guy, and God wanted me to plant a seed, to speak up and say something that just might move him one tiny step closer to Jesus — or eventually lead him to take the plunge and give his life to Christ.

Apparently, this was not the right time and place for anything more to happen than what happened. I did the part God asked me to do in that three-minute encounter with the IBM guy, and the rest is between him and God. As we walked away, I prayed that God would use the seed I cast to open his heart and mind to receive Jesus. And then I was on my way, alert and willing to experience the next engagement that God had for me.

That's what "As You Go" is all about.

As you start reading the chapters ahead, it is my hope and prayer that you will not expect to read more gloom and doom. But that you will consider the stories you read and the information you learn as a wonderful opportunity to invite more people all around you — family and friends and coworkers and strangers — to join you in making the most important decision of their lives: where their souls will spend eternity.

It's not that life's so short; it's that eternity is so long.

My hope is that, just as it was for me, this story will serve as a wakeup call — that life is to be lived to the fullest and the Gospel will be shared intentionally and relentlessly with the enthusiasm and urgency that it deserves. I realize that the word "Gospel" means "Good News", but I never could understand why the message of salvation is called the "Good News". ***It's the GREATEST NEWS ever!***

PART 1

Jesus Said "GO"!

If you don't do it, who will?

"Therefore, go and make disciples of all nations, baptizing them in the name of the Father, and the Son, and the Holy Spirit, and teaching them to obey everything I have commanded you".

Matthew 28:19

"The Gospel is only Good News, if it gets there in time."

Carl F.H. Henry
American Theologian

Carl F.H. Henry was an American evangelical Christian theologian who provided intellectual and institutional leadership to the neo-evangelical movement in the mid-to-late 20th century. His profound statement on the previous page should wake up any believer who cares about other people and give them a sense of urgency for sharing the Gospel.

"The Gospel is only Good News, if it gets there in time."

Just think of your loved ones and people you care about in this world — family, friends, co-workers, neighbors. Do we really care about where each of these souls spends eternity? It's easy to say we do. But are we willing to get engaged in "showing another beggar where the bread is"? Are we willing to stop being judgmental and start extending our hands in love and grace and mercy? Are we willing at the right time and place to ask the difficult, but unavoidable, questions about what they believe and are putting their hope in? Are we willing to be authentic and vulnerable and tell the real stories about our own lives, our triumphs and tragedies?

If you don't do it, who will?

But first I want to remind you what the message of the Gospel really is. To do that best, I want to quote the words from a sermon by Craig Smith, Senior Pastor at Mission Hills Church in Highlands Ranch, CO, which happens to be our home church.

Here is part of what he shared at the Sunday service:

> *"It's the Good News that God loves us so much that He sent His own Son to pay the price for our sins. That the Son of God himself went to the cross to take our place. He rose from the dead, and he offers forgiveness and new life by simply trusting in what He did for us. Like that's good news, right? Are you ever going to hear better news than that? There is no better news!*
>
> *What Paul said to the church at Galatia is 'How did you receive God's spirit? Because you worked really hard, or because you trusted in what you heard?' Now Jesus says, 'Remember what you have heard and what it allowed you to receive.'"*

So, it sounds like Craig is telling us that someone else, namely Jesus, paid for my sin and yours on the Cross — once and for all. ***That's Great News!***

> *"What does trusting in the Gospel allow us to receive? Where do you even start? Like forgiveness, right? Let's just start with forgiveness. All of your sins, everything you have ever done, everything you are doing right now you shouldn't be doing, everything you are going to do in the future and you wish you wouldn't, but you know you are probably going to slip and fall, and it's going to happen. Jesus says, 'Done, forgiven, paid.' All of it. That's the first thing you receive.*
>
> *You receive a relationship with God. The God that flung the stars across the heavens begins to have a relationship with you. And not just a distant relationship. You are adopted as His son or His daughter as a child of the King. You get that by trusting in the Gospel. Not only that: The*

Holy Spirit of God actually comes into you and begins to change you from the inside out.

Everything you always wished you could be in the depth of your heart, knew you could be so much more than you are, God says, 'You have no idea what I made you to be. Your wildest dreams of what you could be, you are just scratching the surface of what I designed you for. And the Holy Spirit is going to come into you and change you from the inside out, and He is going to make you into something you never believed could be true of you.' We get that by trusting the Gospel.

We get eternal life that goes on forever and forever with God — joy, hope, peace, all these things we get by trusting in the Good News of Jesus Christ. Jesus says, 'You are going through the motions? Here's the first treatment plan.' The first treatment for zombie faith is to remember the Gospel and all that it gives us. It's not 'go sign up for another Bible study.' It's not 'read this Christian book' (obviously, he hadn't read this book yet) or 'listen to this Christian music' or 'get a new church' — no, no, no. He says, 'All of those things are fine. They are all well and good, but the first step for treating zombie faith, is remember the Gospel and all that it gives us.'

The goal isn't people coming to church; the goal is people coming to Christ, and becoming the Church. Do you hear me? That's the finish line. Not more people coming to your building. Not more people coming to services. The goal is more people coming to Christ and then becoming the Church. That's why we say at Mission Hills the one thing that drives everything we do is we want to help people take the next step of becoming like Jesus and joining Him on mission. That's all we do. It's all we do in everything we do. We help people become like Jesus and join him on mission. We want people coming to Christ and then becoming the Church itself."

Now Craig is saying that I can have a better life and possibly realize my wildest dreams. Furthermore, I just might receive God's blessings of a joyous, peaceful, purposeful, meaningful life on earth.

"You can't look upon this call to action as a tremendous burden and weight on you that you suddenly are accountable for the salvation of every person in your sphere of influence. Only God Saves, not you. But God not only wants us to do our part, but also commands us to be His hands and feet in a fallen, secular world. We can relax about the results; God's in charge of that. But we must take action in countless ways through our lives to be the best possible representatives of who Jesus is and what He has done for us."

I believe that God wants you and me to do whatever we can — by His Holy Spirit and the power of Christ in us — to share this message with the nations at a moment in history that desperately needs to wake up to the ***Good (Great) News*** before it's too late.

I Can Make a Difference

Jimmy Carter, former President of the United States, has said, "I have one life and one chance to make it count for something... My faith demands that I do whatever I can, wherever I am, whenever I can, for as long as I can with whatever I have to try to make a difference."

As I write this last paragraph, it sounds arrogant to think that God has chosen a normal person like me to take on such a grandiose task. But isn't that the way God has accomplished His purposes throughout history? Almost exclusively, the characters in the Bible that God chose for His plan were the ones who seemed least likely to be qualified and capable of the task at hand. Moses talking to Pharaoh, David slaying a giant called Goliath, and Mary giving birth to the Son of Man.

My attitude about the writing of this book is that if God wants me to take all of the time and effort to complete His instructions and if He wants me to do this to impact only one person on the planet for the Kingdom, then it will be worth every hour I spent being obedient to God when He told me to write a book called ***As You Go***. Even if that one person turns out to be me.

But I want to be clear about this: These stories are not meant to show how smart and cool I am and what a great Ambassador for Christ I am. It's about what God has orchestrated in my life simply because I told Him I was willing to be used by Him in every way and everywhere possible for His honor and glory. And I believe God will use you in unimaginable ways if you will only let Him.

I hope you will let Him and join me as a member of the team called Christ's Ambassadors, ***As You Go***.

But you can't do that if you choose to stand on the sidelines or sit in the stands as a spectator. You've got to "get in the game," put on your gear to "go into battle," and "stand in the gap" to reach the unconvinced and disciple the believers, ***As You Go***. And we need to do it urgently!

Whether Jesus is coming back next week or 10,000 years from now is not really our concern. Only God the Father knows when it will be — not even Christ knows. The reason for our urgency should be because we don't know how many more days our family, friends, neighbors, and co-workers have until their last day on earth, and for that matter, none of us knows when our last day will be. However many days we have left, we need to make them count for the Kingdom.

We should get on about the business Jesus commanded us to do shortly before He ascended into heaven: to "go and make disciples of all nations, baptizing them in the name of the Father and of the Son and of the Holy Spirit and teaching them to obey everything I commanded you."

The following quote by Theodore Roosevelt really describes it best, and I love it:

> *"It is not the critic who counts: not the man who points out how the strong man stumbles or where the doer of deeds could have done better. The credit belongs to the man who is actually in the arena, whose face is marred by dust and sweat and blood, who strives valiantly, who errs and comes up short again and again, because there is no effort without error or shortcoming, but who knows the great enthusiasms, the great devotions, who spends himself for a worthy cause; who, at the best, knows, in the end, the triumph of high achievement, and who, at the worst, if he fails, at least he fails while daring greatly, so that his place shall never be with those cold and timid souls who knew neither victory nor defeat."*

Who will join me, As You Go?

1

Facts Tell the Story!

We need to know the truth.

"If you hold to my teaching, you are really my disciples. Then you will know the truth and the truth will set you free."

Matthew 6:17

"It takes strength and courage to admit the truth."

Rick Riordan
New York Times Bestselling Author

"We must have strong minds, ready to accept facts as they are."

Harry S. Truman
Former President of the United States

One of the most startling and disturbing facts about the current state of Christianity from my research for this book is this: ***Less than 3% of Christians are obeying Jesus' command in Matthew 28:19 to "go and make disciples."***

Here are some additional troubling facts about our current world according to several reputable research organizations:

Christian Beliefs

- 60% of Christians believe it is "extreme" to attempt to convert others to your faith. (Barna Group)
- 51% of churchgoing Christians in the U.S. are not aware of the Great Commission, and another 25% have heard about it but can't recall its exact meaning. (Barna Group)
- 70% of all young people who grow up in church leave by their 20s. (Barna Group)

Today there are more Christian movies, books, music, seminars, conferences, leadership training, contemporary churches, and small groups than ever before, yet we are losing ground in this country. All around us, it looks like things are literally "going to hell in a handbasket."

Believers and followers of Jesus Christ are not telling nonbelievers about the Good (Great) News. It's as simple as that!

Is it any wonder that non-Christians find it almost impossible to see any difference between their behaviors and beliefs and those who claim to be Christians and followers of Christ? And, unfortunately, many times what they do see from some Christians screams of hypocrisy. "Do what I say, not what I do." Even young kids pretty quickly figure out that this parenting approach does not work.

Sharing Jesus with the World

As far back as 1923, the British theologian Smith Wigglesworth is quoted as follows:

> *"The reason the world is not seeing Jesus is that Christian people are not filled with Jesus. They are satisfied with attending weekly meetings, reading the Bible occasionally, and praying sometimes. It is an awful thing for me to see people who profess to be Christians lifeless, powerless, and in a place where their lives are so parallel to the unbelievers' lives that it is difficult to tell which place they are in, whether in the flesh or in the Spirit."*

If Wigglesworth made this observation almost 100 years ago, what would he say about Christians today? My guess is that he would say the same thing, but he would be shocked and appalled at how much further the Christian community has slipped away from being filled with Jesus and sharing Jesus with the world.

The reason the world is not seeing Jesus is that Christian people are not filled with Jesus.

On the one hand, there seem to be fewer and fewer believers as a percentage of the population living a fully integrated life in Christ that is evident to people around them — sharing love, grace, and mercy with others, serving instead of being served, giving rather than only taking.

On the other hand, because there are fewer Christians living a fully integrated life, how much easier it will be for our Christian worldview, biblical values, positive attitude, and loving behavior to shine like a bright beacon of hope in the depraved and broken world where we live in today's culture. When you are loving and kind to the condescending jerk in the office, when you display peace and calm in the face of financial difficulties in the business, or when you help and serve others unselfishly without expecting anything in return — people will notice big time, and they will be wondering if that's really what a Christian is like. Because if it is, then they will likely want to find out how to get some of that for themselves.

Chad Hovind, Christian author, commented in CBMC's Living Proof Adventure: "Let's make our lifestyle and our values so attractive that people want to know what makes us different. How is it that we have meaning and purpose? You told me about a marriage struggle you were having a while back. It seemed like your values helped you in that. That's the kind of thing that gets people asking questions."

And we should be prepared and willing to share it with them, ***As You Go***.

Living It Out, *As You Go*

Key Points to Remember

- Only 3% of believers are sharing their faith with anyone.
- The younger generations are more disconnected from God than ever before, and we as Christians are losing ground.
- Be led by the Holy Spirit and quickly ask the Lord how He wants you to respond to the person or situation He has brought across your path.

What Will I Do?

1. What could I do to have even the slightest positive impact on these numbers?

    ____

    ____

    ____

2. Under whose authority am I to "GO"?

    ____

    ____

    ____

3. What would be a good prayer to prepare myself, ***As I Go***?

    ____

    ____

    ____

2

God Told Me To!

"I want you to write a book."

"A time to tear, and a time to sow; a time to keep silent, and a time to speak."

Ecclesiastes 3:7

"It takes strength and courage to admit the truth."

Rick Riordan
New York Times Bestselling Author

"When God speaks to you directly, you must pay attention and take action to be obedient."

Victor Dawson
Ambassador for Christ, Author of **As You Go**

A few years ago in February, I was invited by a dear friend and colleague, Paul Johnson, with CBMC (Christian Business Men's Connection) to accompany him on a trip to South Africa for two weeks. We were there to conduct a seminar on Leadership Coach Training near Cape Town and Johannesburg/Pretoria. I had been involved with CBMC for over 20 years at that time and was active in the ministry in the U.S. and several countries internationally.

My wife, Nan, joined us on this trip, and it turned out to be one of the most memorable travel experiences of our lives. The country was beautiful, and the people we met were so kind and genuine.

On the long flights to South Africa from Denver, I had plenty of time to think about what God might want me to share, in addition to helping Paul teach the principles of leadership coaching. I suspected that the CBMC team in South Africa would ask me to speak to a number of local teams in and around both cities during the weekdays, in between the two seminars held on Friday evening and Saturday. And my suspicions held true as I was blessed to meet a lot of men involved with CBMC there and share what God had put on my heart.

So, in the relative quiet of a long flight, I began to make an outline of what I might share. Over recent years, God had given me the opportunity to share my faith and the Gospel with many people in various countries around the world and in the U.S. Some of the best stories are in this book. He had gradually drawn my attention more and more to Matthew 28:18-20, commonly referred to as "The Great Commission." And I began to wonder and question why more Christians were not following this command from Jesus shortly before He ascended into Heaven.

A Command, Not a Suggestion

From what I read in that verse and from listening to people much more knowledgeable about the Bible than I was, this statement from Jesus was a COMMAND, not a suggestion. I believe that's something to pay very close attention to if you are a follower of Jesus Christ.

Who was Christ talking to when He issued that command? Was He talking to pastors or seminary professors, or church and para-church leaders, or evangelists? He was issuing this command to EVERY SINGLE BELIEVER! That means you and me and everyone who professes to believe and accept Christ as their Savior and Lord.

This statement from Jesus was a COMMAND, not a suggestion!

As I started to follow this commandment, I began to notice more and more that I seldom, if ever, ran across another believer who was following this command to "go and make disciples of all nations." And when I asked some questions and did some research, I was shocked and dumbfounded to find out that the best information available indicated that less than 3% of Christians were telling other people about Jesus and "teaching them to obey everything I commanded you" (verse 19). And I don't mean often; I mean very little, if ever. How could this be? More about that later.

Full-Time Ministry

The outline I developed first asked the question, "How many of you are in full-time ministry?" In my first meeting in South Africa of almost entirely businessmen, the answer was no one. And the answer has been the same every time I've ever asked that question. Occasionally, there will be a youth pastor or other minister in the group, and they will raise their hand. I admit the question is a little bit of a play on words. Most people think of pastors, missionaries, youth leaders, and other church and para-church employees as the only ones who are being paid by an organization to be in "ministry."

I was able to speak to about 10 groups of men on my trip to South Africa, and each time the reaction and response was virtually the same.

But if I want to be obedient to what Jesus commanded in Matthew 28:18-20, then I must be in full-time ministry, even though I am a businessman and don't get paid a dime by any religious organization. And so I am in full-time ministry, 24/7. Well, except maybe when I'm sleeping a few hours most days.

The rest of the outline was about what it would look like if you choose to obey The Great Commission? Who would you become? What would you do? How would you equip yourself for this wonderful life experience?

Nan and I arrived in Cape Town at about 5 p.m. on a Thursday evening and were met at the airport by the CBMC Director for South Africa, Frik van Rensberg and his lovely wife, Letitia. They took us to their home and welcomed us with a wonderful dinner. As we were finishing the evening and planning to try to sleep for a few hours after 27 hours of flying with a stopover in Dubai, I asked Frik about the plans for the next day. He replied that we needed to leave the house at about 5:45 a.m. to drive 45 minutes to a meeting of CBMC men in Cape Town at a local church. Well, OK then; let's hit the ground running after a short nap!

With the awful effects of jet lag and the great excitement about being there, it was hard to get much sleep. But we got up early as planned, showered and dressed, and headed to our meeting across town.

As we arrived at the large church and went upstairs to a big coffee shop on the second floor, we noticed that there was a large group of young people in the lobby of the church praying together. My first thought was, "Well, there goes the mistaken idea that millennials never get up and out of the house until about 10 a.m."

But if I want to be obedient to what Jesus commanded in Matthew 28:19-20, then I must be in full-time ministry.

The group of CBMC guys that assembled that morning totaled 20 to 25 men. After about 15 minutes for some initial comments from Frik and Paul, the group in the lobby broke up, and many of them headed up to the coffee shop for their favorite latte and some breakfast. It became very noisy in the coffee shop, and we decided it would be best to split into two smaller groups and for Paul to lead one and for me to share with the other.

I began to briefly share my thoughts on The Great Commission and being in full-time ministry, and the discussion was going well. I was pleased that this group was showing a lot of interest in my message. When we were nearing the allotted time for our meeting and I was encouraging everyone to be in full-time ministry as businessmen, the thought occurred to me that I should give them a challenge. Since we had also discussed the importance of reaching the younger generation that morning, my challenge to them was for each man to go and meet at least one of the people in the coffee shop and connect with them for a couple of minutes. They all sat there like stone figures with fearful expressions on their faces. Keep in mind that these guys are successful businessmen, and the people I wanted them to talk to were most likely Christians. After a couple of uncomfortable minutes waiting for someone to move, I got up and proceeded across the room. I had noticed two young men when they first came in who were probably college students and were sitting at a table by the window. So, as I got up, the Holy Spirit led me to believe that they should be the ones I should engage with.

As I approached their table, they looked up, and I simply said, "Good morning, how are you guys doing?" I told them my name, and we shook hands and they told me their names. Then I said, "Were you with the group down in the lobby praying this morning?"

"Yeah, sure," they replied.

I responded, "Great, I'd love to hear more about your group. Is it OK if I pull up a chair for a few minutes?" That's all it takes most of the time to engage people in conversation.

We had a nice chat for about 10 minutes, I also told them who I was and why I was here, and we exchanged contact information, which I shared with one of the local CBMC leaders. As I came back to my group of guys, they looked astounded, like they couldn't believe what they just witnessed. I shared with them about the conversation I just had with the two young men and challenged each of them to have at least one of these encounters in the next week. Sadly, I seriously have my doubts about whether a single one of these men met this rather simple challenge.

After that first Friday morning, I was sure that I was onto something useful and something that God had given me to share with others. I shared the message nine more times on this trip, and it seemed well received each time. When I returned to the U.S., I also had the opportunity to speak to several other groups and begin to hone the message.

They all sat there like stone figures with fearful expressions on their faces.

Signs of Trouble

Let's move forward a little over a year after our South African trip to the scene at the LAX airport in Los Angeles. I had just flown on a small prop plane from Carlsbad, CA to LAX (Los Angeles). The flight was running late, so I was in jeopardy of missing my connection back home to Denver. Down the stairs by the plane I went, grabbed my roll-on bag and strapped my briefcase to the side of it, and then started to jog up the three ramps to the terminal. I continued to walk fast, almost running, to get from Terminal 1 to Terminal 2, where my next flight was minutes from leaving without me. About halfway there I felt very winded and had some tightness in my chest, somewhat like after a run up a hill when your chest is burning. No sharp pain or numbness, so hopefully I was not about to have a heart attack. I stopped to catch my breath and then slowly walked to the next gate, realizing that if I missed the flight, then so be it. I made the flight after all.

When I returned home that Tuesday afternoon, I immediately called my cardiologist, who I had been seeing for several years as a preventive measure. He was on vacation out of the country, but his PA suggested that I have a nuclear stress test as soon as possible, and they scheduled me for Friday morning of that week. After the episode at LAX, I was fairly sure that I would flunk my treadmill test at the cardiology center. Surprisingly, I did fine, and the technician told me they would call right away if there were any problems, but not to worry if I did not get a call for a couple of days. When there was no call on Friday, I was feeling optimistic that things might be fine with my heart and that the shortness of breath was a different issue, maybe just me being a little out of shape at 60 years old.

My Wife, the Lioness

By Tuesday of the next week, my wife had also returned home from California, and I was getting on a flight that afternoon for an overnight trip to Salt Lake City. Nan called me as I was sitting on the flight ready to takeoff and asked if I had heard anything from the cardiologist. I had not, and she got very excited and concerned. She hung up and called the doctor immediately. She spoke to the nurse first and got her concerned enough that she got the doctor on the phone. He had been out of the country the previous week, and that's why we had not gotten a call about the results of my stress test. So, he quickly pulled up the file and said to Nan, "The results look as good as the one we did on him two years ago."

Quite surprised but undaunted by his opinion, she asserted, "I don't care what the test shows. I have been trying to tell you for over a year now that there is something wrong with my husband, and you won't listen to me!"

Hesitantly, he replied that the only thing he could do next would be a heart catheterization, where they inject dye into my bloodstream and insert a camera to take pictures of my heart and the arteries and valves. Nan said, "Great, he will be back tomorrow evening from Salt Lake City, and we will see you on Thursday morning."

As you will learn in the next few pages, thankfully Nan had just saved my life!

On Thursday morning we checked in at the cardiology center for the heart catheterization procedure. A very nice nurse about our same age greeted us and got me ready for the procedure. Nan is generally quite inquisitive, so she was asking the nurse many different things about what was about to happen. One question she asked was "Do you ever have any cases where, once they have the results of the heart catheterization, it's serious enough that they take the patient straight away to the hospital?" The nurse replied that in the 10 years she had been there, she knew of about three or four such cases. Well, that sounded good, or so I thought.

In the operating room, I was awake as the doctor inserted a large needle into the artery in my right arm to begin the procedure. Sometimes they will insert the needle in one of your legs and run the line with the camera up to your heart through your groin. I was pleased they had chosen the other route.

There were three large video screens or monitors hanging above me on the left side, and the doctor was watching them closely as he inserted the camera and began the documentary video and picture-taking exploration of my arteries and heart valves. The main part of the procedure took only about 30 minutes. Near the end of that time, the doctor looked up at the screen and stared for a minute, then said to me, "We have something here we need to talk about." Oh, great! That sounded to me like the line from the movie "Apollo 13" when Tom Hanks, playing astronaut Frank Borman, radios after an incident with the spacecraft on the way to the moon and says, "Houston, we have a problem."

As you will learn in the next few pages, thankfully Nan had just saved my life!

The doctor pulled one of the monitors down closer for me to see and showed me a white area along one of the arteries near the entrance to my heart. It turns out that it was my left main artery, called the widow-maker (apparently for a good reason), which was over 90% blocked. Wow, I was a ticking time bomb and could have ended up like the lady in the San Diego airport at any minute! What I learned later is that when the left main artery closes down and you start having a heart attack, you need to be standing in the lobby of the emergency room at the hospital and you still might not make it.

I was taken back to the recovery room, where the doctors explained to my wife and me the dire situation. The only good news was that there had not been any damage to my heart so far. They recommended Dr. Myles Guber at Porter Hospital nearby to do the surgery, scheduled an appointment to see him on Friday morning and then scheduled my open-heart surgery for the following Monday morning. We later learned that Dr. Guber is one of the finest heart surgeons in the country, and we were comforted to know I would be in good hands.

I had considered over the weekend that even though open-heart surgery has become quite commonplace, Monday could be my last day on this earth.

As the two doctors at the cardiology center are giving us final instructions before sending me home, I asked if I could take a short ride down to Colorado Springs (about 45 minutes) to attend my grandson Jonah's third birthday party. They said it would be best if I stayed at home. Then they said to my wife, "If he has any more symptoms, don't try to drive him to the hospital. Just immediately call 911." The news was already sounding quite serious, but now they were making us more concerned. And if the doctors' instructions weren't disturbing enough, on the way out the door, the nurse leaned over close to us and said, "You guys take care. I'm really surprised that they're allowing you to go home." Well, isn't that special!

Peace from Jesus

The reason for waiting until Monday might have been the fact that it was Father's Day weekend and everybody had plans other than doing my surgery. So, I went home and sat quietly watching the U.S. Open golf tournament for two and a half days. My grandson, Jonah, came up to visit me at home and I gave him his first set of golf clubs. It was so exciting to see my new golf buddy trying to hit plastic golf balls in the backyard.

Over the weekend there was probably too much time to wait and think about what might be next. Lots of prayers and conversations about how my life had suddenly taken a drastic turn. But given the seriousness of my condition, I felt an amazing sense of peace and calm — maybe more so than at any time in my life.

There can be only one explanation for that peace: It had to be Jesus! While I had remained calm over the weekend (well, for the most part), I suspected that as it came time for the medical staff to wheel me away to the operating room, things would get more emotional. I had considered over the weekend that even though open-heart surgery has become quite commonplace, Monday could be my last day on this earth. But I was calm about that because I knew that my soul would be going straight to Heaven to be with Jesus for the rest of eternity. And while I wanted to stay longer, I was at peace that God was in control. So, at the appointed time, I got hugs and kisses from Nan and my daughter, Amanda, and my son, Michael, and did not get emotional as I thought I would. They did, but not me. I was at peace either way it turned out. And anyway, what could I do to affect the outcome at this point?

Four hours later, I was in the recovery room, trying to wake up from the anesthesia (don't you just hate that?). It's worse than the fog I get when I enter the shopping mall with my wife for the afternoon. You're alive and you're pretty sure you'll still be alive a few hours later, but the experience can be torturous.

I felt an amazing sense of peace and calm — maybe more so than at any time in my life.

Member of "The Zipper Club"

The surgery had gone really well, although I didn't know it at the time. Even though the doctor told me it went well, what else was he going to say? "Sorry, I screwed it up pretty badly"? It would be five days later before I was beginning to believe it. I developed hiccups the first day after the surgery and essentially had them for three days. It's apparently not uncommon to have hiccups after open-heart surgery, but normally they can control it with medication rather easily. Not so for me; I was special. Imagine having a hiccup every 10 seconds for the better part of three days with a 12-inch incision in the middle of your chest. Sleeping becomes quite a problem, and that gets old in a hurry. With the stitches on both sides of this 12-inch incision looking like a zipper, I was now able to be a member of "The Zipper Club."

My family and I did learn why this operation is called bypass surgery. One of the reasons is that the doctor is going to use arteries from another part of your body to bypass the artery near the heart that has the blockage. That makes sense. Often they use arteries from your legs, but in my case, they used two mammary arteries from my chest, which are supposedly much better and stronger. All these years, I didn't even know I had mammary arteries.

But during the surgery, Nan and my family learned a second, amazing reason it's called bypass surgery. One of the Operating Room nurses came by the waiting room about halfway through the procedure and informed them that I was doing well and that everything was going as planned. Then she said that another nurse would come by to talk to them and let them know after they had restarted my heart. SAY WHAT? Everybody on the planet probably already knew that from taking that Cardiac Surgery Class in high school, but for some reason, that step in the process never really occurred to any of us. So, the other reason it's called by-pass surgery is that they put you on a heart/lung machine to literally bypass your heart with blood and oxygen and then stop your heart to do the new plumbing work. Wow — now we know!

I had to stay an extra day in the hospital while they got rid of the hiccups, but finally on Saturday morning I was released to go home.

God Speaks to Me

Upon our arrival home, my three little girls, Maddy, Emma, and Lily — who are a dachshund, a Chiweenie (dachshund and chihuahua mix), and a Yorkie, respectively — were ecstatic to see me again and jumped and barked and danced like I had been gone for years. I was almost as excited as the girls to be home still walking, talking, and breathing, but I couldn't dance like they could yet. Of course, they quite often do that when I've been gone to the grocery store for an hour, but you may know how animals can sense when something is wrong, and they sensed it immediately. For the next three weeks, they were attentive to my every move and lay on the bed or beside the bed to make sure I was OK.

Early on Monday morning, one week almost to the hour after the surgery, I was feeling a bit better, so I ventured out onto the back patio in the shade and cool air of a mid-June, sunny day in Colorado to have my "quiet" time of prayer and reading the Bible, just as I do almost every day.

My prayers to the Lord obviously started with tremendous praise and thanks for how He had saved my life through the love and tenacity of Nan and how well the surgery had gone. I remember thinking that God must have something else for me to do, that He was not quite finished with me here on earth yet. So, I asked Him, "Lord, I believe that you still have a purpose for me in this world, and while I don't know if it's for the next 2 months or the next 25 years, it sure would be awesome if You could tell me more about Your plan."

I remember thinking that God must have something else for me to do, that He was not quite finished with me here on earth yet.

Immediately in the still and quiet early morning, I heard Him through the Holy Spirit say, "I want you to write a book."

"Oh really, are You sure about that?" I thought. And just like so many characters in the Bible that God spoke to, I was making excuses and trying to tell Him that I wasn't too sure I could write a book. I mean, throughout my business career I have written a lot of letters, reports, proposals, and marketing communications. But a book? I'm not an author, right?

Is anyone else thinking how crazy it is that I'm arguing with the Creator of the Universe about what He is asking me to do? It sure seems nuts now, but it was just my first reaction at the time.

Then the Holy Spirit said, "Yes, I want you to write a book and call it 'As You Go'." Further, He said, "You know that information you have been sharing in the last year about what it looks like to be in full-time ministry and live out Matthew 28:19? That's what the book should be about."

Wow! I will say it again: Wow!

At this point, I'm sure that some of you are thinking, "Yeah, right. God spoke to you directly and gave you instructions?" You might be praying to God, but do you truly believe that God hears and answers your prayers? The Creator of the Universe hears your prayers; OK maybe so. But God speaking almost audibly through the Holy Spirit directly to you with specific instructions? I've read it in the Bible, and I've heard a few other people report such an encounter, but for somebody like me?

Then the Holy Spirit said, "Yes, I want you to write a book and call it 'As You Go.'"

Well, it really happened, and I have no doubts about the source and authenticity of the message. In fact, it was the second time God had spoken to me this way in two years. So, you might think, having received a clear message and direction from God, that I would have jumped on this task and written a book immediately, right? Sorry, it didn't happen that way. And it had nothing to do with whether or not I believed this message was from God. I previously expected and have now confirmed that writing a book is a very difficult and time-consuming process, especially for a first-timer.

In all the amazement and excitement of this intimate, personal contact with the King of Kings and Lord of Lords, I forgot to ask a couple of important questions. The first question was "How many pages do You want this book to be?" And secondly, "When do You want me to finish writing it?" I did get started making an outline and thinking through some of the content and stories to include in the book, but the actual writing of the words was challenging, to say the least. I have done a lot of writing in business and consulting and I think I'm a fairly good written communicator. But writing and publishing a book for public consumption, that's a different animal all together.

After a couple of years, writing a few pages here and there on long airplane flights to Asia or Europe, and trying to juggle all the other aspects of my business and personal life, I finally asked God through prayer to answer those two questions I had forgotten to ask. He answered me with a plan for disciplined writing and a serious commitment to finish the book within six months.

And it worked. It still was a challenging, time-consuming process, but a lot of things worth doing seem to be that way. If it were so easy, I guess everybody would be doing it.

I hope you are enjoying this expression of God's will for me and my lifetime purpose and will make the practical ideas suggested in this book part of your daily life, ***As You Go***.

Living It Out, *As You Go*

Key Points to Remember

- Jesus' commandment in Mathew 28:18-20 is not a suggestion; it's a directive to be done, ***As You Go***.
- We are commanded to be in full-time ministry to love others and share our faith.
- With a little practice, it's fun and easy to meet new people and talk to others about your faith and their salvation.

What Will I Do?

4. Has God ever spoken to me through the Holy Spirit? If not, why not?

 ____

 ____

 ____

5. If I do not communicate intimately with God, what could I change that might allow that to happen more often?

 ____

 ____

 ____

6. Is there something important, maybe huge, that God has already shown me, but I don't know what to do or where to start?

 ____

 ____

 ____

3

Are You In Full-Time Ministry?

Jesus appointed you as His Full-Time Ambassador!

"We are therefore Christ's ambassadors as though God were making the appeal through us. We implore you on Christ's behalf: be reconciled to God."

2 Corinthians 5:20

"The Christian ideal has not been tried and found wanting; it has been found difficult and left untried."

G.K. Chesterton
English writer, poet and philosopher

I have been privileged to speak and share my story with business people in small groups, at retreats, and various other gatherings in countries in Asia, Africa, Europe and the U.S. After my introduction as a business owner, entrepreneur, and servant leader, one of the questions I like to ask first, as I originally did in South Africa, is this: "How many of you in this room are in full-time ministry?"

Now, when I ask that question, I do so with a bit of a play on words. Because most people associate the term "full-time ministry" with someone who is working on a full-time basis for a church or para-church organization and is paid by that organization to do their work. Ministers, senior pastors, priests, youth pastors, missionaries, and many other job titles are the ones that fit into this category called "being in full-time ministry."

As a businessman who loves Jesus and wants to share Him with others — whenever and wherever I go, meaning "***As You Go***" — I have been frustrated for years when I hear well-meaning Christians ask the following question: "Victor, since you've already spent decades doing business, when are you going to quit your job, go to seminary, get into full-time ministry, and start doing some important work for God?" How's that for a judgmental statement, oftentimes from somebody who barely knows me and what I do?

Christian Ministry

I believe that far too many in the Christian world have this distorted view of what it means to be in Christian ministry. They think that if you really want to serve God, you need to be a pastor or a missionary. It's like you're somehow a second-class person in the eyes of God and the world unless you are involved in the world's perspective on "being in full-time ministry." Sadly, too many churches and Christians view successful business people as greedy, worldly, and unclean. At least until it's time to pass the collection plate and ask this successful business person to give generously to the church's operating budget, or the building fund to upgrade the sound system, or to add a new wing on the church for the kids' ministry.

Please forgive me for my harsh words above, because I realize that there are many churches and organizations that do not intentionally have that view of business. But still far too many do.

Even though I'm a businessman, my answer to the question I often ask at the beginning of a talk is that "I'm in full-time ministry" — every hour I'm awake and maybe even sometimes when I'm asleep (not quite sure how that last part works). The fact of the matter is that as a businessman I can reach as many or more people in the world than my pastor can. And I can reach people with the ***Good (Great) News*** who won't even give the pastor the time of day. As soon as that person meets "the Reverend Dr." or "Pastor Whoever", they know exactly what to expect they'll hear from him. And most people in our culture are pretty sure they've heard that message before and know what being a Christian is all about — even if they really know very little.

In my case, I can reach the factory owner or manager in China, or one of my customers or clients, or one of my suppliers, or other people in various fields in the marketplace. And I can sneak up on them. And I don't mean that in a deceitful way. They just initially won't see me coming to tell them about Jesus. I can spend time to build a trusting and respectful relationship by showing the love of Christ in me. As time goes on, I can "raise the flag" about my Christian faith, and then look for God to create opportunities for me to share the Gospel more fully. I can reach people that have no interest in talking to a pastor or going to church. And that's a lot of people. Plus, I get to do my ministry seven days a week, instead of mostly just on Sunday.

I can spend time to build a trusting and respectful relationship by showing the love of Christ in me.

I actually might have the opportunity and privilege to have even greater impact than seminary-trained Christian pastors and leaders. This statement is not meant to be a criticism of pastors or a prideful statement about me. God might allow me to lead a business owner with hundreds or thousands of employees to Christ, who will, in turn, run his business in a different way, starting to multiply the love of Christ with his employees, customers, and suppliers. And then the spouses and children of some of these people will be positively impacted for the Kingdom, and then maybe some of their friends and extended family and neighbors. I get chills running up my back just thinking about it as I write this paragraph.

And guess what? I'm no big deal. **Anyone can do this with a desire to follow the command of Jesus in Matthew 28:19, *As You Go.***

WDJD – What Did Jesus Do?

What did Jesus do when He started his three-year ministry on earth? He called ordinary people in business in the marketplace — fisherman, tax collector, doctor. He didn't call the priests and seminary-trained people. And He did not preach exclusively in the temples and synagogues. Jesus made 132 public appearances recorded in the New Testament, and 122 of them were in the marketplace. He spent virtually all of His time in the marketplace spreading the ***Good (Great) News*** and making disciples in some way with everyone He came in contact with.

Dr. Darryl Bock, Executive Director of Cultural Engagement for the Center for Christian Leadership at Dallas Theological Seminary, in an interview with Guy Rodgers, President and CEO of Pinnacle Forum, talks about their focus at the Center being on how theology applies to culture. "In my view, that's a more sophisticated way of saying it's about how my faith and biblical worldview should be a full-time experience in all areas of my life, especially at work."

Guy responds in the interview with this great comment: "My ministry is my work, and my work is my ministry."

Furthermore, Dr. Bock says,

> *"Maybe where God has placed you is exactly where He wants you to be at this moment in time. And maybe you should look at your business or employment differently and see your employees or coworkers as your flock, and not just people to manage or work with. Relate to them, not just from a business perspective, but from a pastoral concern for them as God's children.*

We're all Kingdom priests wherever God has us. So, no matter where God has placed you at any moment in your life, you have the potential — you're actually called to serve the people around you. Loving God and loving your neighbor, and even loving your enemy, is about that kind of service.

Jesus didn't say, "Go into the church and make disciples"; He said, "Go into the world."

When you accept God's sovereignty enough to understand that God has you where He wants you for a purpose, and the people He's put around you for a reason, and the work He has you do is service for a reason — then all of a sudden you don't treat the nine-to-five hours at work the same way. It's not the black hole of your life where you earn money to do all the other things in life you want to do.

Then you realize that 'I'm here for a purpose and a reason, and God has put me here for a purpose and a reason.' And now you're in a different state of mind, not only to do your work but to interact with people and actually engage in what is real relational ministry.

I like to send out the message that God has designed an evangelistic program for the Church that the Church has largely ignored: And that's where people work, and the way they do their work, and the way they view their work. Because that evangelistic program actually

> *connects to the creation mandate. God made every human being to do and be, and that mandate was to tend the garden in the world in which He's put us, and in that way, we are called to work together and serve one another well, male and female."*

Dr. Bock adds, "We all have a unique set of contacts and connections, right where God has placed us. And then you say, 'Use me.'" Jesus didn't say, "Go into the church and make disciples"; ***He said, "Go into the world."***

We're beginning to get some traction in the Body of Christ on this idea, but we still have a long way to go.

Ambassadors for Christ

Paul, writing in 2 Corinthians 5:20, makes it abundantly clear that if we are followers of Christ, then we are His ambassadors, Christ's ambassadors. And furthermore, that God is making His appeal to the world through us. What an awesome responsibility and opportunity!

What is an Ambassador? A dictionary definition would say the following: "an accredited diplomat sent by a country as its official representative to a foreign country" or "a person who acts as a representative or promoter of a specified activity." Wikipedia defines an ambassador as "an official envoy, especially a high-ranking diplomat who represents a state and is usually accredited to another sovereign state or appointed for a special and often temporary diplomatic assignment."

What are some of the key words used in these definitions? *Representative, diplomat, accredited, official, special, high-ranking, and promoter.*

So, let's think about it in this context: God, the Creator of you and the Universe, has appointed you to a high-ranking position in His organization to represent Him in this foreign land (Planet Earth, which is not our home) on a temporary basis. "Temporary" meaning from the time you accept Christ until the moment He brings you home to Heaven. It's a position of great respect and responsibility.

What are Ambassadors of countries on Planet Earth charged with doing? The easiest way to think about it is that when you see or interact with one of these ambassadors of a country, you expect to see the country they represent. The way they look and dress and talk and act are all things they do that should accurately represent the country they represent. And part of their role is communications and negotiations on behalf of their nation. And they are often on public display, as their lives and activities are watched closely by the media and the foreigners.

What does it mean to be Christ's Ambassador? Doesn't it mean essentially the same things as the ambassador of a country but with a much higher purpose of eternal perspective? Doesn't it mean that Christ has given you a high-ranking diplomatic position and directed you to be fully engaged in this "foreign land" with people that need to know and accept Him as their Savior, or to know Him better and more fully?

An Ambassador gives a very high priority to his work and his role. While his faith and his family may ultimately come first, he spends most of his time focused on his ambassadorial role.

How are we doing in fulfilling that high-ranking position for Christ as His Ambassadors? I must admit that I have failed miserably at this role quite often. Why, it took me the first 50 years of my life just to truly understand that Christ had appointed me to this important position in the Kingdom and to find out the job description for this role. And I believe that most Christians do not fully understand the significance and importance of 2 Corinthians 5:20, when Paul writes, "We are therefore Christ's ambassadors as though God were making the appeal through us. We implore you on Christ's behalf: be reconciled to God."

Just like the Great Commission, we think that this scripture must apply to someone else. How in the world could I be considered an Ambassador? That is a special position only given to a limited number of people in the organization. Well, not in God's world. He appointed every one of us believers to be Christ's Ambassadors. Being an Ambassador for Christ was not a suggestion; it was a command. And even though there are billions of these ambassadors in the Kingdom, it does not, in any way, diminish the power and influence of this role.

Part of the reason that there needs to be so many Ambassadors of Christ appointed is that the job is so huge to represent Christ in the world and to reach the unconvinced. Possibly another reason might be that He has given each of us a unique set of gifts, talents, and experiences. He needs Ambassadors in business, the military, education, sports, churches, medicine, government, entertainment, and politics.

And the list goes on and on.

One of the biggest challenges that believers and

non-believers face is the compartmentalization of our lives — family, work, church, home, hobbies, sports. And so we tend to focus on only that compartment when we spend time there. We don't recognize that we can be full-time Ambassadors for Christ in every one of these areas of our lives.

The Mind of Christ

But that's how I see it, and that's what this book is all about. It's about changing your perspective on who you are in Christ, what positions of power and authority God has appointed you to, and how you go about living out that life and mission, ***As You Go***.

In Matthew 28:18, the verse just prior to the Great Commission, Jesus says, "All authority in heaven and on earth has been given to me." And then He is essentially saying in the next verse, "Therefore, I'm going to give you ***ALL*** that authority to live out My command, ***As You Go***."

And we can carry out this command with the mind of Christ. In 1 Corinthians 2:16, Paul writes, "For, 'Who has known the mind of the Lord so as to instruct him?' But we have the mind of Christ."

Furthermore in Philippians 2:5-8, Paul again writes about this subject: "In your relationships with one another, have the same mindset as Christ Jesus: Who being in very nature God, did not consider equality with God something to be used to his own advantage, rather, he made himself nothing by taking the very nature of a servant, being made in human likeness. And being found in appearance as a man, he humbled himself by becoming obedient to death — even death on a cross!"

Having the mind of Christ means we "look at life from our Savior's point of view, having His values and desires in mind. It means to think God's thoughts and not think as the world thinks." It is a shared perspective of humility, compassion, and dependence on God.

I hope that when you have finished reading this book, every person will raise their hand to the heavens and declare that you are in full-time ministry and that you are a full-time Ambassador for Christ, ***As You Go***.

Living It Out, *As You Go*

Key Points to Remember

- Jesus' commandment in Mathew 28:19 is not a suggestion; it's a directive, or a commandment.
- Jesus was commanding all believers to carry out the Great Commission.
- An Ambassador's role is to represent his country in a foreign land. As an Ambassador of Christ, you are His representative here on Planet Earth.

What Will I Do?

7. How can I change to become a better Ambassador for Christ? Do others recognize me as one?

___

___

___

8. Do I believe that I have been given "the mind of Christ"? If yes, what does that mean? If no, why not?

___

___

___

9. What does it mean to have "ALL authority in heaven and on earth?

___

___

___

4

Two Great Commands from Jesus!

They are not suggestions.

Jesus replied: '"Love the Lord your God with all your heart and with all your soul and with all your mind.' This is the first and greatest commandment. And the second is like it: 'Love your neighbor as yourself.' All the Law and the Prophets hang on these two commandments."

Matthew 22:37-40

"The Great Commission is not an option to be considered; it is a command to be obeyed."

J. Hudson Taylor
British missionary to China

Owner's Manual

The Bible is filled with many wonderful commands and ways to live our lives as described by Jesus. I like to think of it as "The Owner's Manual" for me and every other human being. You can take any problem or issue you face in life and find the answer about what to do or how to behave in the Bible, especially in the New Testament. God gave us His Word so we could get to know Him better and understand how life works best in the world God created.

So, in Matthew 22:36 when the Pharisees tried to give Jesus a trick question by asking Him, "Which is the greatest commandment in the law?" He gave them the perfect answer and defined two of the most important activities God wants us to do. He said quite simply to "Love God and Love Your Neighbor." We refer to that scripture as The Great Commandment.

Jesus later raised the bar even higher in Matthew 5:44 and in Luke 6:27 when He commanded us to also "love our enemies." Really? It's hard enough to love all the people in the category of my neighbors, which obviously means more than just the people who live on my street. But my enemies — people that are hell bent on hurting me, driving me out of business, or just being hateful and vengeful — are you serious?

Learning More Truth

Del Tackett is the creator of The Truth Project. If you have not viewed the 12 Tours or Episodes in this small-group study, I would highly recommend you do so. It is a masterful work done for the purpose of exposing us to more truth about who God is and the truth He has revealed to us in all of the various areas of life, such as philosophy, anthropology, justice, family, business, science, government, and community.

While The Truth Project was viewed by over 15 million people in numerous countries around the world and had significant impact in teaching valuable information to Christians about God and a biblical worldview, Del admitted that it fell short in explaining what to do now that we know more truth. Has it done any good to learn a comprehensive, systematic biblical worldview? Has it resulted in the people of God bearing fruit and impacting the culture? I'm sure it has, but Del believes the Lord has made it clear what we should be doing with that worldview. That will be the heart of his new series, the **Engagement** Project.

The following paragraphs are slightly edited excerpts from my notes of Del's talk to a group of Christian leaders regarding "What Is God's End Game? What does God want us to do"? (Before using this information in the book, I asked for Del's permission, and he graciously granted it to me.)

Serious Opposition

According to Del, we live in difficult times — a time when all of the social powers are opposed to a biblical worldview. They don't just sit on the other side of the stadium and watch; now they boo at us and even attack us. Virtually all areas of our culture are opposed to a biblical worldview: academia, media, Hollywood, music, comedy, movies, and in many cases, the government and the courts.

Furthermore, business is now wielding a greater power to force us to conform. For instance, the sports business world is taking an increased role in trying to force its worldview by threatening to move tournaments out of states that don't conform, or other businesses are threatening to move their operations in order to force conformity.

We live in difficult times — a time when all of the social powers are opposed to a biblical worldview.

Here is the most important part of what Del shared:

> *By their actions, they want to force us to believe that there is no absolute truth, except what the culture says is true. The issue of male and female is a perfect example. The culture is trying to force us to believe that a person is not born as one or the other but can decide for themselves whether they are male or female. Many would argue that "male" and "female" are just social constructs. I live in Colorado, and have a lot of rabbits in our neighborhood, and I'm quite certain that they have not arisen because of a social construct.*
>
> *There probably isn't anything in human life that is more real than the fact that we exist as male and female. Yet some of the most intelligent of these species seem to be wrestling with whether male and female are real things. And they even have a fear of speaking that truth out loud, even if logically they agree. The culture is increasingly unable to speak absolute truth or say anything that might appear to be truth beyond the*

individual.

The Nature of God

"Think about what God did in Creation. When He created the plants, He did not create the plants to simply look good in the Garden. No, when He created the plants, He did something quite astounding — quite amazing actually!

He created the plants and He equipped them, He empowered them, and then He set them free to bear fruit and to multiply. And then He delegated out of His own nature, to a plant, the responsibility, the capability to produce new life. Do you think God could have created new plants every day? Why did He do it this way?

The reason is because of the crown jewel in the nature of God and who He is.

And when God created the animals, male and female, He did the same thing. He equipped them, He empowered them, and then He sent them to be fruitful and multiply, that the animals themselves might bring forth new life.

And then He created Adam and Eve, and He equipped them, He empowered them, He charged them, and sent them that they might multiply and bring forth good fruit.

The culture is increasingly unable to speak absolute truth or say anything that might appear to be truth beyond the individual.

All About Me or Agape

> *"We've all heard the quote 'God is Love.' In Psalm 136 the words 'His Love Endures Forever' is repeated in every verse. That phrase can be translated as loving-kindness, or grace, or goodness, or loyal love, or merciful kindness, or steadfast love of God — and it's everlasting! The apostle John often referred to it as Agape Love.*
>
> *In our culture today, this kind of love is not what we normally think about as love. We say things like 'I love that movie,' or 'I love that song,' or 'I love that dress,' or 'I love that car,' or 'I love these tacos.' This love is all about me, my story, and my script. What we have done with the cherished word 'love' is to make it all about me. I love all these things because they enhance my script.*
>
> *True agape love can be defined as 'the steadfast, sacrificial zeal that diligently, objectively, seeks the true good of another.' How opposite is that to a love that is focused on itself? It's about as opposite as you can get, because it has nothing to do with my script and everything to do with another person.*
>
> *So, when you say, 'I love you' to your husband or wife, it should be more than just an emotional feeling or infatuation like the Hollywood kind of love. When you say those words to your spouse or your children, what you should really mean is 'I sacrificially and diligently want to seek your true good.'*

At the beginning of this chapter, I mentioned that the Greatest Commandment that Jesus gave is in Matthew 22:37-40, "to love God and love your neighbor." Paul reminds us again in Galatians 5:13 and in Romans 13:9 to "love your neighbor." Jesus then added another: to "love one another." All three of these are focused on the command to love.

Bob Goff in his New York Times bestselling book, *Everybody Always*, writes, "Being engaged is a way of doing life, a way of living and loving. It's about going to extremes and expressing the bright hope that life offers us, a hope that makes us brave and expels darkness with light. That's what I want my life to be all about — full of abandon, whimsy, and in love."

Love My Neighbor

Who is our neighbor? The Greek word for neighbor is *plēsion*, and the definition is "the one who lives near" I believe it could mean more than just the people that live in the houses or apartments near you. It should also include others in your community or church or social group or coworkers (where we spend as much or more time together than we do at home with our families and certainly with any other neighbors). The guy in the office next to you at work certainly lives near you for many of his waking hours.

So, we need to ask ourselves, "How well do you think we're doing?" Can we say, "We have a sacrificial zeal that diligently seeks the true good of the people that live next door"? Sadly, most Americans don't even know their four closest neighbors. How can this be? The Holy Spirit moves Paul to say that all of the commandments can be summed up in this one thing: Love your neighbor. The people that providentially live next to you and across the street. And we don't even know their names and definitely have not engaged with them to build any kind of meaningful relationship.

A friend of mine in Las Vegas recently shared a funny but sad story about neighbors. He had lived in his house for three years with his wife and two kids. They were in the process of moving out and loading up the moving truck when their next-door neighbor came out of his garage, waved at him, and shouted, "Are you our new neighbors?" Shame on both of them.

"That's what I want my life to be all about — full of abandon, whimsy, and in love."

But I can't criticize because we had a similar thing happen to us. Nan and I had a young couple that lived next door to us for about six years. We didn't know them extremely well, but they had been to our house numerous times for a BBQ or a party, and we had all helped each other out with tools or referrals, etc. One day I was working out in the front yard when Craig came out of his garage and headed over to talk about something with me. In the course of the conversation, I asked how Erika was doing since we hadn't seen her lately. Craig shared that they had been divorced for 18 months. I was stunned! I couldn't believe that I had been so oblivious to what was going on with friends living next door to us that we didn't know anything about this sad news! It sure was a wakeup call for me.

Who Is Supposed to GO?

The second Great Command that Jesus gave us is the Great Commission. In Matthew 28:19 when Jesus said, "Go and make disciples of all nations," who was He talking to? Who was supposed to do this?

Most people think Jesus must have been talking to missionaries. They are the ones that quit their jobs, go to seminary, learn a foreign language, and move halfway around the world to some third-world country to share the Gospel and lead people to the Lord. And for people who are called to do that, I praise God for their desire to serve in that way.

Since 99.9% of us are not interested in such a radical change in lifestyle and do not feel called to the mission field in a third-world country, we generally write off the Great Commission as something meant for someone else.

"What if the Great Commission was supposed to be fulfilled one neighbor at a time by the people of God?"

Or maybe Christ was talking about pastors and church leaders. After all, those are the people that have the training and knowledge about "going and making disciples," right? Sure, Matthew 28:19 should be part of their teaching and preaching and leading of the church. I believe it's God's design that pastors have the responsibility to equip the followers of Christ in the Church to carry out this mission, but not to be the only ones doing it.

What if the Great Commission was supposed to be fulfilled one neighbor at a time by the people of God, building a deep relationship with the people who providentially (you didn't pick your neighbors) live next to you?

Del makes the point that this commandment is in the context of families; "love your neighbor" is inherently a family vision. And that begins with men, who are leading their family to build relationships with their neighbors. What would it be like if all of a sudden, when you have family prayer time, your little girl begins to pray for Mrs. Smith across the street, after we just found out that Mrs. Smith hates God because her husband recently died of cancer? She has been bitter at God, and nobody comes to see Mrs. Smith.

I really think that Jim Petersen of the Navigators hit the nail on the head when he said, "We look at the Great Commission as some onerous task that we have to fulfill, but it really is an opportunity for charging our lives with meaning."

Jesus was talking to all believers in both of these Great Commands — the Great Commandment and the Great Commission. His message is as clearly stated as anything in the Bible. If you want to be obedient to Christ, these are not suggestions for you if you feel like it; they are commands.

Engagement is what God wants us to do in order to obey His two Great Commands.

These are imperatives that bring honor and glory to God and pay huge dividends to you and the people whose lives you touch in obeying these two commands, ***As You Go***.

Living It Out, *As You Go*

Key Points to Remember

- I like to think of the Bible as the "Owner's Manual" for me and every other human being.
- The culture around us is increasingly unable to speak absolute truth.
- Engagement is what God wants us to do in order to obey His two Great Commands.
- God's love is the Agape version, which can be defined as "the steadfast, sacrificial zeal that diligently, objectively, seeks the true good of another."

What Will I Do?

10. Can I say, "I have a sacrificial zeal that diligently seeks the true good of the people that live next door?"

    ____

    ____

    ____

11. How can I show Agape Love that seeks the true good of another?

    ____

    ____

    ____

12. How can I get better and much more engaged in the two Great Commands?

    ____

    ____

    ____

5

Why Don't More Believers Share?

Less than 3% is shameful!

"I pray that your partnership with us in the faith may be effective in deepening your understanding of every good thing we share for the sake of Christ."

Philemon 1:6

"I learned that courage was not the absence of fear, but the triumph over it. The brave man is not he who does not feel afraid, but he who conquers that fear."

Nelson Mandela
Former President of South Africa and anti-apartheid revolutionary leader

We're all familiar with the list that someone supposedly compiles from a survey of average people called the "Scariest Things in Life." Generally, the top three items include things like death, speaking in public, and flying.

At some point earlier in my life, these three items would have definitely made the top 5 or 10 scariest things in my life. But now I love to fly all over the world, I enjoy and desire to do public speaking, and death is just part of my eternal journey.

I'm convinced that if this survey was given to only Christians and one of the possible answers was "Sharing My Faith with a Non-Christian," that answer would easily top the list of the scariest things in life. Hence, 97% of believers don't follow the command of Jesus in Matthew 28:19 to "go and make disciples." They seldom, if ever, are willing to tell other people about the ***Greatest (Good) News Ever***!

Phil Manginelli, founder and pastor of The Square, a new church plant in Atlanta, Georgia, said in the CBMC Living Proof Adventure videos on lifestyle evangelism: "We have this picture that God is up there somewhere, and we're running around down here on earth all alone with all of the people that don't know Jesus. The thing that makes us most uncomfortable isn't the idea of giving up our money or even giving up parts of our lifestyle; the thing that makes Christians most uncomfortable is the idea of sharing their faith. So often we approach it like God watches us from a distance to see how we'll do instead of actually being right in the middle of it with us. Sometimes we go too far; a lot of the time we don't go far enough. And somewhere, maybe in the middle between these two extremes, is what Jesus had in mind for the Great Commission."

And as you may remember from the Barna research mentioned in Chapter 1, 60% of Christians now believe that sharing your faith and trying to convert another person is "extreme" behavior and should be avoided.

If only 3% of believers are telling others about their eternal salvation and the way to have a relationship with their Creator — while Satan and the culture are working overtime to steal, kill, and destroy — is it any wonder that Christianity is losing favor and even being attacked in our culture today?

Consider this: What if you had discovered the cure for cancer? Would you tell anyone? Absolutely! If you had a child or grandchild born, would you tell anyone? Of course, you would! If you won the Powerball lottery, would you tell anyone? (OK, you might not want to tell too many people about this.) If you got engaged to be married, would you tell anyone? Of course, you would! What if you got a big promotion at work, would you tell anyone? Of course, you would. And how would you tell other people? "Oh, by the way, this minor little thing like having a grandchild happened in my life today, and you're probably not interested." Heck no! We would want to scream it from the rooftops. We would share this special news with great excitement and enthusiasm.

But when the most significant event in our entire lives occurs — deciding whether our souls will spend eternity in heaven or hell — we clam up and keep it a secret.

I could keep going with all manner of special events and changes in our lives that we can't wait to shout out loud and tell the world about it, or at least a lot of family, friends, and coworkers (even strangers at the grocery store). But when the most significant event in our entire lives occurs — deciding whether our souls will spend eternity in heaven or hell — we clam up and keep it a secret.

50 Big "Buts"

Here is a list of the Top 50 Reasons, in no particular order, why people don't share the ***Good (Great) News*** of the Gospel. See if you can find at least 8 or 10 of your own reasons or maybe add a few new ones to this list.

1. But I don't know enough about the Bible.
2. But I can't defend what the Bible says.
3. But what if this person knows more than I do about religion?
4. But I don't know anything about the other major religions.
5. But someone might ask me a question I can't answer.
6. But I might get rejected or judged.
7. But I might be ridiculed for being a Christian.
8. But I don't have enough Scriptures memorized to quote to people.
9. But sharing my faith might affect my job.
10. But my neighbors might not like me anymore, and I won't be able to go to the block party.
11. But I don't know how to start a conversation.

12. But I don't have enough time.
13. But the weather conditions are not right.
14. But I can't explain how Jesus rose from the dead.
15. But some people don't even believe in God, let alone Jesus.
16. But I might be thought of as a hypocrite.
17. But my favorite TV show is on.
18. But I need to do my Fantasy Football picks.
19. But I'm just not in the mood.
20. But I have too much work to do.
21. But I need to spend time with my kids.
22. But it's such a beautiful day today.
23. But it's rainy and cold outside.
24. But I need to check Facebook.
25. But I deserve a break today.
26. But I haven't had any training.
27. But what does this have to do with the 21st century?
28. But it's too boring.
29. But what if there's a question about Leviticus?
30. But people won't like me if I talk about Jesus.
31. But I just don't have enough money yet.
32. But can't I just let my life speak for itself?
33. But I'm not very well spoken.
34. But I just can't get motivated.

35. But what if God won't do what I ask?
36. But isn't that the pastor's job?
37. But I just don't know where to start.
38. But this is just not my gifting.
39. But what if I get the stories of Barnabas and Barrabas confused?
40. But the timing is just not right.
41. But is it legal to share my faith in public or at work?
42. But I've made a lot of mistakes in my life; I don't have any right to talk to someone else about God.
43. But what if someone responded positively and I don't know what to do next?
44. But why would anybody want to listen to me tell them about God?
45. But shouldn't people just discover God for themselves?
46. But I'm afraid I'll mess it up and push that person further away from God.
47. But I'm going to be late getting home from work for dinner.
48. But I never know which person I should talk to.
49. But I might not be invited to family events.
50. And finally: But I really don't want people to know I'm a Christian.

That's a lot of buts!

Fabien Bouchard of Christian Refuge produced a great video describing some of these "buts." He says, "These 'buts' get in the way of us living a consistent and authentic life for Jesus. God has given us simple directions — if we learn it, if we share it, if we teach it, and live by it, then God gets glorified, people benefit, and we get blessed. That's the 'why' behind what we do. And if your 'but' is bigger than your 'why', then you need to make your 'why' bigger or shrink your 'but'."

Consider Your Whys

Here is a short list of important reasons **"Why"** you should eliminate the "Buts" and focus on what the benefits are:

1. You might have a dramatic impact on a person's life by leading them to accept Christ as their Savior.
2. You will be storing up treasures in heaven.
3. You might make a new lifelong friend.
4. You will be faithful and obedient to Christ's command in Matthew 28:19.
5. You will be thrilled to see God show up in your life and use you to reach others for the Kingdom.
6. You will encourage and inspire others to share their faith, ***As They Go***.

How Much Do We Care?

As believers, do we not care enough about our closest friends and family to be actively involved in sharing this ***Good (Great) News***? Nan and I have a dear friend that we have known for over 30 years. She is a lovely lady and like family to us. She grew up in a different country and probably was exposed to the Protestant church in her youth. She married a man with a different faith and immigrated to the U.S., where we first met them. They have three wonderful children but were recently divorced. This lady is a kind, giving, and loving person with strong values of right and wrong. Yet, to my knowledge, she has not accepted Christ as her Savior.

As believers, do we not care enough about our closest friends and family to be actively involved in sharing this Good (Great) News?

I have tried a couple of times to share the Gospel with her with gentleness and respect, but she still believes that there must be different paths to God for good people. Sadly, a lot of people have this belief.

Therefore, it is my belief that without accepting Christ's free gift of eternal life, her soul will spend the rest of eternity in hell when she dies. That fact or truth is deeply disturbing! Why wouldn't we want one of our dearest friends to be with us in heaven? Why wouldn't we do whatever it takes to give her the opportunity? But sadly, many people do not want to offend someone and take a risk of losing them as a friend; I understand that. But the stakes for eternity are too high!

Please recognize that if I have prayed for our dear friend and done my best to present Christ to her through my life and words with gentleness and respect, and she is unconvinced and rejects salvation, then I can be at peace about it.

God is the one who saves, not me. But I must be bold and use every opportunity to witness to this dear, special friend.

And we must also conquer our fears and eliminate the "buts" to at least reach out to those we love, ***As We Go***.

Living It Out, *As You Go*

Key Points to Remember

- Only 3% of believers are sharing their faith; why aren't the other 97% being obedient to the Great Commission?
- When the most significant event in our entire lives occurs — deciding whether our souls will spend eternity in heaven or hell — we clam up and keep it a secret.
- There are a lot of "buts" that get in the way of us living a consistent and authentic life for Jesus.

What Will I Do?

13. What "buts" are my favorites, the ones I regularly use? Do I have more?

____

____

____

14. Who are my closest friends and family that aren't believers yet, and what can I do to help them understand the ***Good (Great) News***?

____

____

____

15. What can I do to overcome my fears about sharing my faith?

____

____

____

Summary

The Process So Far — Let's Review:

1. **Jesus said "GO"!** — Only 3% of believers are following the commandment by Jesus to "go and make disciples", The Great Commission. What about you?
2. **When God speaks to you,** follow His instructions to the best of your ability.
3. **Full-time Ambassador** — Change your mindset to be in full-time Christian ministry and be a full-time marketplace Ambassador for Christ, regardless of your work or vocation.
4. **Live out The Great Commandment and The Great Commission:**
   a) Love God, Love Your Neighbor, and Love Your Enemies
   b) Share the ***Good (Great) News*** of the Gospel, As You Go, and "make disciples of all nations... teaching them to obey everything I have commanded you."
5. **Don't let the "buts" get in your way** and keep you from obeying the instructions of Jesus, your Lord and Savior.

PART 2

What Does "As You Go" Look Like?

Prayer and Intentionality are always involved.

"This, then, is how you should pray: 'Our Father in heaven, hallowed be your name, your kingdom come, your will be done, on earth as it is in heaven.'"

Matthew 6:13

"His intent was that now, through the church, the manifold wisdom of God should be made known to the rulers and authorities in the heavenly realms."

Ephesians 3:10

"You get what you intend, not what you hope for."

Chuck Blakeman
Author and Founder of The Crankset Group

What did Jesus mean in Matthew 28:19 when He said "Go"? What am I talking about in this book when I say, "***As You Go***"?

It's very simple; let's not try to complicate it. "***As You Go***" means when I see my neighbor outside doing yard work, I say "hi" and start a conversation. It means when I'm standing in line at the grocery store, I'm engaging with the clerk, or the server at a restaurant. It means talking with my coworkers and customers and suppliers who I spend a huge portion of my waking hours with. It means engaging with the person sitting next to me on an airplane or bus or train. It means when I'm playing golf or attending a sporting event. It means when I'm spend time with family and friends at a social gathering.

It means *All the Time, Everywhere!* Having your radar frequency connected with God and doing what He commanded you to do — **Love Him and Love Your Neighbor, and Go and Make Disciples.** And then when there is a blip on your screen, you pay attention, engage in whatever way the Holy Spirit leads you, and keep going ***Every Day***.

You just need to say, "God, I'm not necessarily able, but I'm willing. Please use me to share You and Your Love with everyone I meet."

In Isaiah 6:8 the prophet says, "Then I heard the voice of the Lord saying, 'Whom shall I send? And who will go for us?' And I said, 'Here am I. Send me!'"

Yes, send me! Send me, *As I Go*!

6

Always Pray First

You may be the only Jesus to someone.

"Rejoice always, pray continually, give thanks in all circumstances; for this is God's will for you in Christ Jesus."

1 Thessalonians 5:16-18

"I pray because I can't help myself. I pray because I'm helpless. I pray because the need flows out of me all the time, waking and sleeping. It doesn't change God. It changes me."

C.S. Lewis
British writer and theologian –
The Chronicles of Narnia and Mere Christianity

Praying for God's Help

Almost every day, I pray and ask God to lead me to people that He wants me to share the Gospel with or people that need to be discipled. And it's amazing how God will answer that prayer and bring people across my path that need to be shown the love of Jesus. And He will be thrilled to do the same for you.

On one occasion I was flying back to Denver on a very early flight after spending time in Houston on business. I sat down in the aisle seat, and there was already a young man sitting by the window, with an empty seat between us. After we took off, I reached in my backpack and pulled out a well-worn copy of my Daily Walk Bible and started to have my quiet/prayer time and read the daily Scriptures and lesson in my Bible.

The young guy did not seem to want to engage in conversation, preferring to lean against the window and catch a few more minutes of sleep. When I finished my reading, I laid the Bible in the empty seat next to me. Soon I noticed that my aisle companion was glancing over at the book. Finally, he said, "What's that book all about?" I shared that it was my daily Bible reading that I normally did every morning.

He seemed interested, and we engaged in conversation along the typical lines of "What kind of work do you do?" "Where are you from?" "Do you have a family?", etc. My new friend was Tim, and he lived in Denver and had been visiting his parents for the weekend in Houston.

I shared with him about my business and my family and also told him that I lived in Denver. Then I mentioned that I had been involved in a Christian men's organization called CBMC (Christian Business Men's Connection). He said he had grown up in the Catholic Church and was a Christian. Then he asked me to explain more about CBMC. So I told him that we focused on reaching unconvinced business people and then discipling the believers.

He suddenly had an astonished look on his face, shook his head, and let out a quiet chuckle with a big smile on his face. He said to me (I guess just to be sure he wasn't dreaming), "So you help guys to be more mature in their faith, seriously?" I replied, "Absolutely, I've been doing that for many years and it's been a really great experience."

Then he shared the reason for the head shake and the chuckle: "You may find this hard to believe, but I've been feeling like I need to get more connected with my faith and grow as a Christian. So last night as I went to bed, I prayed and asked God if He would bring somebody into my life who could help me do that. And here you are, sitting next to me on this flight a few hours after my prayer. I'm just amazed that God answered my prayer so quickly!"

"How cool is that," I was thinking to myself with a big smile on my face! So we talked further, and I explained that I would be honored to help him do life and grow in his Christian faith, and that we should meet for coffee the next week and devise a plan.

And we did! We ended up meeting every two weeks for a long lunch and went through a discipleship program from CBMC called "Operation Timothy." It turned into a great experience for both of us. He shared some things about his dad that had been very challenging for him, and I was also able to talk about the difficulties I had with my dad. We talked about business and how he was handling his work and the interpersonal relationships he had within the company. But most of all we talked about Jesus — who He is and what He's done for us and what He's shared with us about the best way to do life on Planet Earth.

"I'm just amazed that God answered my prayer so quickly!"

We've all heard about the power of prayer. So it should be no surprise that prayer is the first step in carrying out the Great Commission. I'm completely convinced that if you want to follow this command of Jesus and get more engaged in living out and sharing your faith, God will help you in ways you can't even imagine. So, ask Him to bring someone into your path each day, someone who needs a smile and a kind word of encouragement, someone who needs to feel the love of Christ through you, someone who needs to hear the ***Good (Great) News***, or someone who needs to be discipled.

Are You the Reason We're Here?

It may not happen as fast as it did for Tim and me, but if your prayer is sincere, I believe God will bring them to you.

Nan and I know a wonderful couple from Raleigh, North Carolina, who are always asking God to bring people to them that they can share the love of Christ with, ***As They Go.*** Patrick O'Neal is a former President of CBMC USA, and we had gotten to know him and his lovely wife, Tina, at various meetings and functions around the world.

A few years ago, Pat and Tina were traveling to Africa for CBMC International to teach leaders from several African countries about the principles of evangelism and discipleship.

This story they shared with me embodies the ***As You Go*** attitude: trusting God for what happens, looking for divine appointments everywhere, and being willing to open their mouths and share their faith in Christ whenever and wherever the opportunity arises. In other words, they have embraced their appointment as Ambassadors for Christ to "therefore, go and make disciples of all nations."

After being in Zambia and South Africa for about 10 days, they were ready to fly back home to North Carolina from Livingston, Zambia, through Johannesburg, South Africa. They had finished a day earlier than planned, but when they tried to change their flight, the airline wanted to charge $800 each to make the change. They quickly prayed about it and not only felt that it would not be good stewardship of the finances, but also that God was directing them to stay overnight. So, they stayed overnight in Livingston, a city they had never been to before. As the day unfolded, they began to understand that God had a different plan for them that day.

They booked a hotel next to the airport and began to ask different people — the baggage handler, the hotel clerk, a couple in the airport and later the waitress in the restaurant — **"Are you the reason we're here?"** Although they received some very strange looks, everyone responded, "What do you mean by 'Am I the reason you're here?'" They explained how they had not planned to be in Livingston that day, but God had intervened and changed their plans because they are supposed to tell someone about how much He loves them — "Is it you? Do you know God?"

It wasn't difficult, but it was very, very joyful to experience God at work.

Over the next 24 hours, they proceeded to ask some 10 to 12 people the same question, and they heard some amazing stories and witnessed the power of God as they shared the love of Christ with people. It wasn't difficult, but it was very, very joyful to experience God at work.

They passed out tracts to all — "Steps to Peace with God." They prayed with a restaurant manager. A cab driver told them how God rescued him from alcoholism. They met a wonderful believer, the manager of the taxi cab stands in the airport, who gathered five of her workers and, standing in the middle of a bustling airport, they prayed over one of her workers who said she didn't know Christ. This was after hearing Bekki's (the taxi cab manager) amazing miracle of being healed and surrendering her life to Christ. Perhaps she was the reason they were there. Then there was the missionary couple sharing the Gospel in the airport, and Pat and Tina asked them if they were the reason they were there. They said yes; they were there for them. Because Pat and Tina encouraged them and prayed for their unsaved grown son. And this couple was convinced God sent Pat and Tina there to pray for them to continue the race and that He would draw their son to Himself.

The entire episode was a divine intervention based on our heavenly Father's plan for their trip — it wasn't on their agenda, but it was on His. All they had to do was be willing to participate and to be ready; God did the rest!

Hopefully at this moment you are reconsidering the call the Father has placed on your life to be an evangelist and a disciple maker, someone who makes a proclamation of the truth to those God has entrusted to your care. It is a great adventure, so please don't miss seeing the Father, Son, and Holy Spirit at work through you in ways you would never expect.

It is a great adventure, so please don't miss seeing the Father, Son, and Holy Spirit at work through you in ways you would never expect.

Let me also tell you of a recent story where God inspired and encouraged Pat right in the middle of a trial of physical suffering. Remember that as believers, Jesus told us that we are going to experience suffering. But He also said it would be joyous because we know it doesn't last. After all, we know the end of the story, and it is glorious beyond comprehension without any pain or suffering, tears or fear, death or mourning, according to Revelation Chapter 21.

We've Been Stoned

For many years, Pat and I have had something in common that I would not wish on my worst enemy. We have both dealt with several kidney stones, which really can upset your apple cart for several days. Passing a kidney stone has been described as the closest thing to natural childbirth by a woman that a man can experience. After watching the birth of my two children, I can unequivocally agree with the previous statement.

In Pat's case, after experiencing a wonderful Christmas with family, his old "friends" (the stones) decided to make an appearance once again joined by a kidney infection, and shortly after that, another serious intestinal infection. All of which together put him in the hospital for three days. A Bible study group he's in with 8 to 10 other men had just finished 1 and 2 Peter. Among other things from the chapter, they discussed how we are going to suffer as Christians. It might be financial, physical, emotional, persecution for our faith, or even the loss of loved ones.

"Love each other as I have loved you."

This teaching was fresh on his mind as he entered the hospital, so he began to ask the Lord to show him why he was there, in addition to hopefully getting healed. It didn't take long to see God's providence in allowing him to be at the hospital. First, there was a male nurse named Bill who looked at him strangely when Pat asked him if he was the reason he was there. This led to a conversation about how it's possible to know God personally through His Son, Jesus. With Tina praying as she sat beside him listening, they asked Bill if he would be open to reading "Steps to Peace with God." After some conversation he took the tract and said he would read it. Several days after getting out of the hospital, Pat delivered some follow-up material to Bill, and he, together with three other doctors and four nurses, are on their prayer list since they also were open to receive materials about how to have a personal relationship with Christ, who offers us living hope as our Savior.

Bear Much Fruit

These stories prove the power of God at work in us when we are surrendered to Him and desire to be true followers and worshipers of this magnificent Savior, Lord, and King. He wants to use each one of us in His plan and purpose for our lives to bring Him glory and for Him to complete the joy we can experience in His presence. In John 15 we see the Lord's clear encouragement, promise, and warning as His followers. In verses 7 and 8, Jesus says, "If you remain in me and my words remain in you, ask whatever you wish, and it will be done for you. This is to my Father's glory, that you bear much fruit, showing yourselves to be my disciples."

And in verses 11 and 12, He continues, "I have told you this so that my joy may be in you and your joy may be complete. My command is this: **Love each other as I have loved you.**"

While the examples above are those opportunities specially created by God to share our faith, I want to remind you that every day we are on a missionary journey, prepared in advance by the Lord. We need only to focus on our real purpose and be sensitive to how the Spirit is working in us and through us. That purpose is to worship the King, bring Him glory, and be about building His Kingdom.

Chad Hovind, speaking in the CBMC Living Proof Adventure series, says this:

"The bulk of the world is in the darkness. Even in America, there is a huge unreached people group. We send money for missionaries to go to unreached people groups. Meanwhile, Monday through Sunday, we live in an unreached people group. You are the missionary that God has sent to the most unreached people group, the unbelievers in the United States. Instead of saying to them, 'Come to our Christian subculture,' how about instead we become the light to the darkness and say, 'Let me bring to this environment what real integrity looks like, what real humility looks like'? That's the stuff that's attractive to people."

...an authentic Christian: a person that you can see "Christ in them, the hope of Glory."

God has placed each of us in the middle of people He loves and cares for, and we are to build relationships and then be about showing people Jesus, right where He has placed us. I encourage you to learn how to ask powerful open-ended questions to help draw you into others' lives. Then tell them about how you see life and why you have hope.

Let me encourage you as Philemon 1:6 says, "I pray that you may be active in sharing your faith, so that you will have a full understanding of every good thing we have in Christ." In other words, God uses the sharing of our faith as part of maturing us in trusting and growing in Christ. The second part of sharing our faith is becoming a disciple maker after we have been discipled.

For most of us, it's not too hard to imagine that someone in Africa might not have seen and heard Jesus proclaimed. The truth is that the same thing happens all around us. Even in America — where Christian beliefs are shared in books, movies, music, TV, social media, the Internet, churches, retreats, conferences, and more — many people have never personally seen or engaged with an authentic Christian: a person that you can see "Christ in them, the hope of Glory."

A lot of Americans think they know all about Christianity; they've seen it and heard about it for years. Unfortunately, many of the images they see and the impressions they get are done in the most offensive ways — judgmental and self-righteous, without gentleness and respect.

So, God wants you to pray first, then step out in faith, and He will bring people for you to meet and share with, ***As You Go***.

Living It Out, *As You Go*

Key Points to Remember

- Almost every day, I pray and ask God to lead me to people that He wants me to share the Gospel with or people that need to be discipled.
- Prayer is the first step in carrying out the Great Commission.
- God will bring people to you to share the Gospel, if you will only ask Him to.
- You may be the missionary that God has sent to the most unreached people group, the unbelievers in the United States.

What Will I Do?

16. Can I make a daily commitment to pray that God will open doors for me to share?

    ____

    ____

    ____

17. Can I ask someone, "Are you the reason I'm here?"

    ____

    ____

    ____

18. Am I willing to get engaged and experience the great joy of seeing God at work through me?

    ____

    ____

    ____

7

Use Words Only if Necessary!

Let God's love and light shine for all to see.

"In the same way, let your light shine before others, that they may see your good deeds and glorify your Father in Heaven."

Matthew 5:16

"Share the Gospel at all times. Use words only if necessary."

St. Francis of Assisi
Founder of Franciscan Order of Monks

"Darkness cannot drive out darkness: only light can do that. Hate cannot drive out hate: only love can do that."

Martin Luther King
Preacher and Civil Rights Leader in the 1960s

There seems to be some debate about whether St. Francis of Assisi, an Italian, Catholic monk in the 12th century, actually gave us that quote about how to share our faith. If he did, that's great. If he didn't and no one has any idea where it came from, I'm fine with that, too. The reason I share it is because I believe it succinctly captures the first step after prayer in living out the Great Commission, ***As You Go.***

We've all seen it with our own children or observed it with other people's children: They mimic our behavior. They learn from our behavior. They watch what we do and then try to duplicate it. At least until they get to be teenagers and have realized that they know everything and that their parents are old and out-of-touch. As Mark Twain supposedly remarked about his adolescence, "When I was sixteen, my parents were so ignorant, I could hardly stand to be around them. Now that I'm twenty-one, I can't believe how much they have learned in five years."

We've all seen and experienced it in all facets of life — sports, business, education, relationships, marriage, child rearing, etc. It's a natural part of the learning and growing process, although we definitely need to be careful about whose behavior we are using as our model. That's one of the most serious things to consider about what kind of life you want to live. Simply put: Who are you hanging out with and who do you follow on social media? (But that's another big topic for someone else to write a book about.)

People Are Watching You

One of my mentors was once complimenting and affirming me for the way I was handling the care of my mom, Grace, in her early 90s. After living in the same small town in Georgia for the first 90 years of her life, it became necessary to move her to Colorado to live with us due to a diagnosis of the early stages of Alzheimer's. Caring for an elderly parent with dementia or Alzheimer's is not for the faint of heart. It's one of the most challenging things I've ever done. And without the full help and support of Nan tirelessly caring for her mother-in-law, I don't know how it would have been possible to do this by myself. We sometimes jokingly say that it was the toughest three years of our life. Actually, it was only nine months; it just seemed like three years!

After my mentor had made a few nice comments affirming what I was doing for my mom, he then made a statement that was quite an eye-opener: "One of these days, you'll be really glad you handled this well, because this is most likely how your kids will treat you when you reach this point in life." Hello? I'd certainly never thought about it that way, and I wasn't selfishly trying my best to give loving care to my mom, who had shown me love throughout my life, for that reason. Then he finished by saying, "Your kids are watching how you handle this very closely."

As Christians living in a fallen, secular world, we're generally aware that people are watching us to see how we live out our faith. Is it real and authentic, or is it convenient and hypocritical? Once the world around you finds out you are a Christian, they will be watching you closely. Whether it's at work, in your neighborhood, with your golf buddies, or with other family members, they're going to be eyeballing you.

So, I believe that this old adage is true: "What you do speaks so much louder than what you say." And you and I are sharing our faith in Christ every minute of every day by what we do without saying a word. And believe me: What you do matters a lot. Often without even realizing it, for good or bad, we are sharing our faith with those around us. That's exciting to me most of the time, but all too often it's a scary thought when my actions and behavior are not representative of my faith in Christ.

God Shows Up in China

One of the highlights of my business career was a four-month assignment in Shanghai, China. There's another story near the end of the book that started during this same assignment in China.

About seven or eight months before I started living in Shanghai for this assignment, I had begun working with a new supplier in Nanjing, the old capital of China at first during the Ming Dynasty in the 14th century and again from 1927 to 1949. The young lady who was the liaison for the factory had the English first name of Catherine. She was a very bright and beautiful young woman and was very pleasant to work with. Before living there that Fall, I had met her on two previous trips to Nanjing in the late spring and early summer. Her company was a new supplier for us, and we were constantly in contact by email and phone.

After I started living in Shanghai that Fall, I made regular trips by train, about four hours one way, to visit Catherine and her company to check on the status of our orders and also to visit a couple of other suppliers in the area. Her company was doing a good job manufacturing the items we ordered even though the delivery schedule was tight.

Catherine was engaged to a sharp young man who worked as an engineer. We had been to dinner together a couple of times in Nanjing, and they really were enjoyable to be with. So, a couple of months later, I invited them to come to Shanghai on Friday for a long weekend so Catherine could tour our warehouse and fulfillment facility to learn more about my company and see the products that her factories had produced.

Our driver took me in the company van to pick them up at the train station on Friday morning, and we stopped for lunch on the way back to our facility. Catherine was always curious about me and my family, and I was happy to share pictures and stories with her. I was also very interested in learning more about her life and her fiancé's story.

Then on the way to our facility, Catherine turned to me and asked this amazing question: "Please tell me what you know about God." Wow — how's that for an open invitation to share your faith!

Before I tell you how I answered her question, it's important for me to share something that had been happening for months before that moment: I had been praying for her. I had been asking God to give me an opportunity to share Christ with her. I had been praying that God would prepare her heart and mind to listen to me and receive Him.

After spending a few hours at our facility that afternoon, I again accompanied them in our company van to the hotel that we had arranged for their overnight stay. On the way there, we talked more about business and the status of our orders. We also talked about her role at her company and her desire to one day have her own factory.

With about 20 minutes left in our ride to the hotel, Catherine turned to me and said, "You know what we were talking about earlier? I'd like to talk with you more about that soon." At first I thought she was talking about how to start her own business and what I thought about that. So I told her that I would be happy to give her any business advice that I could. She replied, "No, I mean what we talked about this morning, about God. When are you coming to Nanjing again?"

Go Where God Is at Work

Well, OK then. She is asking me to tell her more about God. How awesome is that? I thought for a second and quickly replied, "I'm planning to come back to Nanjing next Friday and stay over on Saturday. Could we meet then and talk further?" She said that would be great. Honestly, I had no plans or real business reason to be going to Nanjing next Friday, but with an invitation to tell her and her fiancé about Jesus, I was definitely going.

All that next week I was constantly thinking about this invitation and divine appointment that God had given me. I prayed a lot that week for God to prepare their hearts and minds to receive His message and that I would have the right words to say — not my words but His words through me.

Early that next week, two members of my company's management team arrived from Denver to stay until the end of the week. Dennis Scruggs was the CFO and Bill Wilking was the Accounting Manager, and both were fellow believers and dear friends. They were excited to hear about the experience I had with Catherine and her fiancé a few days earlier. Although Dennis had to return to the U.S. at the end of the week, Bill decided to stay a couple of extra days and go with me to Nanjing on Friday.

That Friday evening in Nanjing we met Catherine and her fiancé for a nice dinner and then went to my hotel room to talk. We continued the conversation that we had started a week before about God, and they both had some interesting questions. Such as "What is the meaning of the Father, Son, and Holy Spirit?" I glanced over at Bill, hoping he wanted to field that question, but he slightly bowed his head to pray and left me hanging there to answer.

I shot up a quick prayer for help. My explanation may easily not meet the approval of seminary professors and Bible scholars, but it made sense to me and they nodded with better understanding. I shared that it's about one being with different roles, somewhat like me being a son, husband, father, etc.

Then I gave them a copy of "Steps to Peace with God," a small trac developed by CBMC. We talked about love and sin and salvation, and how Jesus is the bridge, and they were really getting it. At the end of going through this short booklet, I asked this simple question: "Can you think of any reason why you would not want to accept Jesus Christ as your Lord and Savior right now?" They both gave a thoughtful pause and then came back together with a self-assured "NO." So I lead them through the Sinner's Prayer together, while my heart was almost beating out of my chest with excitement.

The four of us all hugged, which is an unusual thing to do in Chinese culture, and then sat back to reflect on what had just happened. Catherine looked over at Bill and explained to him that she was the liaison for her company with many European and American customers. She shared that most of these customers were so demanding, stressed, rude, and hard to deal with, especially if there was any issue or problem.

Then she shocked me with her next statement: "I've been working with Victor for about six months, and I really noticed that there was something different about him. He was always nice to me, and we worked on problems together." I spoke up quickly, "Catherine, that was not me." She looked a bit confused for a moment, and then with a big smile on her face like she knew the answer, she replied, "It was the Spirit." Yes, Catherine, Yes! It was the Spirit!

We have become lifetime friends with Catherine and her family. We don't get to see them very often, maybe every five years, but we'll enjoy our friendship for as long as we can here on earth and then continue enjoying it for all eternity.

Whoever said it first does not matter: Share the Gospel at all times; use words only if necessary, ***As You Go***.

Living It Out, *As You Go*

Key Points to Remember

- Share the Gospel at all times. Use words only if necessary.
- What you do speaks so much louder than what you say.
- Can you think of any reason why you would not want to accept Jesus Christ as your Lord and Savior right now?

What Will I Do?

19. What behaviors do I have that are not a good representation of Christ?

    ____

    ____

    ____

20. What changes can I make in the way I live my life to allow people to see "Christ in me"?

    ____

    ____

    ____

21. How can I do a better job of letting God's light and love shine through me, ***As I Go***?

    ____

    ____

    ____

8

Let God Transform You

A Changed Life is a Powerful Witness!

"Do not conform to the pattern of this world, but be transformed by the renewing of your mind. Then you will be able to test and approve what God's will is — His good, pleasing and perfect will."

Romans 12:2

"Transformation is a process, and as life happens there are tons of ups and downs. It's a journey of discovery."

Rick Warren
Founder & Sr. Pastor of Saddleback Church in CA

"The only person you should try to be better than is the person you were yesterday."

Unknown

When someone at work or in your neighborhood knows you are a Christian, do you think they are watching what you say and do and how you do it?

We just discussed in the previous chapter the power of sharing the ***Good (Great) News*** without using words unless necessary. In other words: letting your talk, actions, and behavior show people something attractive in your life that they want to experience themselves, and it will draw them closer to Christ. And hopefully they will ask you how you can possibly act that way under the circumstances, as Catherine in Nanjing did, because they want to know how to be like that. Then you get an opportunity to share your story and tell them about Jesus. Pretty simple, right?

Do What I Say, Not What I Do

It is simple, but the problem is that my actions and behavior and talk are not always pleasing to God. And so, if I'm not careful, I will come across as a hypocrite or like a person who my friends and co-workers would watch and say, "If that's what it looks like to be a Christian, I don't want any part of it." I can actually make it harder for someone to receive the ***Good (Great) News***, simply by them observing me.

I don't know about you, but for me that's unacceptable. First of all, I want so strongly to be more like Christ, even though I will never reach His level of righteousness, sinlessness, and perfection. Secondly, I want to be a good witness and live a life worthy of a follower of Christ, for my joy and blessing — but more importantly for His honor and glory.

I accepted Christ as my Lord and Savior when I was 17 years old and a freshman at Georgia Tech. I attended a few meetings of Campus Crusade for Christ and prayed the sinner's prayer. But no one came along after that to disciple me or to help me understand what it meant.

Not long after I graduated, I started working for a consulting firm specializing in engineering and manufacturing. Some of the guys that I worked with at that firm and many of the people at the companies we worked for often used bad language and told dirty jokes as a normal way of life. It didn't take me long to start doing the same thing. Now I'm appalled and ashamed about how I behaved back in those days. It seemed quite acceptable in the environment and culture I found myself in, but it was definitely inappropriate and ungodly behavior.

When I finally rededicated my life to Christ at the age of 40 and was discipled by a more mature believer in Houston, this behavior was one of the things (and trust me, there were plenty of others) that I was able to see as wrong and in need of change. So I asked for God's help and went about being more conscious of those behaviors and being determined to stop it. Honestly, I still probably let a bad word slip every now and then, but it is totally different than before and quite noticeable to people around me.

It's not just about changing some bad language and a few habits — it's much deeper than that. It's about transformation. Romans 12:2 says, "Do not be conformed to the pattern of this world, but be transformed by the renewing of your mind. Then you will be able to test and approve what God's will is — His good, pleasing, and perfect will."

OK, that sounds wonderful, but how do I do that? Well, the most important way to do that is to read, study, and meditate on God's Word — the "Owner's Manual" for human beings. And don't just read it once; read it over and over again. Each time God will reveal new insights and understanding as you grow and mature in your faith. There are so many options now for reading the Bible: phone apps like YouVersion, an endless variety of reading and study plans, devotionals, Bible study groups, a Christian mentor or Paul/Timothy relationship, audio and video studies.

Changing Me

But before you do anything, how about praying to God and asking Him to transform you, to show you what needs changing, and to show you how to go about doing it? Since God knew you before He knit you together in your mother's womb, and He has every hair on your head numbered (by the way, it's taking Him less time to keep track of the hairs on my head these days) — He might just know what's best for you and how you can be transformed. You think?

> ***The most important way to do that is to read, study, and meditate on God's Word — the "Owner's Manual" for human beings.***

Another great way to become more Christlike is to find someone of the same gender who you know and trust and is more spiritually mature than you are, and ask them to be an accountability partner for you. Let that person ask you the hard questions about what you're doing and not doing, and consider ways to change your attitudes and behaviors. If you are being discipled or coached by someone, that person could be perfect for providing you with accountability. This approach has worked extremely well for me over the years, and I believe it's something I will need for the rest of my life. I'll never get so smart or knowledgeable or mature that I can stop improving. It's a lifelong journey that we should all be focused on.

As an example of how this personal transformation can impact your ability to share your faith, I have continually grown in trusting God and not being anxious. One of my life verses is Philippians 4:4-7, which says, "Rejoice in the Lord always. I will say it again: Rejoice! Let your gentleness be evident to all. The Lord is near. Do not be anxious about anything, but in every situation, by prayer and petition, with thanksgiving, present your requests to God. And the peace of God, which transcends all understanding, will guard your hearts and your minds in Christ Jesus." I still act human sometimes when serious challenges come, but my peace and calm in the midst of difficult circumstances can often be quite noticeable.

So, when I was working for a company that was in serious financial distress and I had no idea if I would lose my job or the company would go out of business, I was able — by God's grace — to be much calmer and at peace than most people I worked with because I knew God was in control and had a plan for my life. That lack of anxiety would lead a couple of coworkers to ask me how I could be so calm during this scary time. And I could then say, "Let's get together for coffee or lunch soon, and I'll explain." It's that simple.

As I mentioned, this transformation process for each of us should last a lifetime. But do not think for one minute that you need to change yourself into the nearly perfect human being before you get involved in "going and making disciples," ***As You Go***. It's just a cop-out or one of those "Buts" that will keep you from living out the Great Commission. You can do what Jesus commanded all the while you are moving in the direction of Christlikeness.

One of the resources I would recommend to you to become a better Christian and marketplace ambassador is called the "Ten Attributes of an Effective Marketplace Ambassador." This study and video series were developed by CBMC and has proven very helpful to believers desiring to be transformed. The link to this program is listed in the section at the end of the book on Additional Resources.

The last — or maybe the first — thing that you need to do to be transformed is to be willing and committed to allowing Christ to do that work in you. It's an inside job, so let Him work to develop you into the person God made you to be, ***As You Go***.

Living It Out, *As You Go*

Key Points to Remember

- Let your talk, actions, and behavior show people something attractive in your life that they want to experience themselves.
- The only person you should try to be better than is the person you were yesterday.
- Be willing and committed to allowing Christ to transform you from the inside out.

What Will I Do?

22. Should I be reading, studying, and meditating more on my "Owner's Manual"?

____

____

____

23. What can I do to become a better person today than I was yesterday?

____

____

____

24. Will I pray for God to transform my life according to His plan and purpose for me?

____

____

____

9

Be Alert and Available at All Times

God wants to use your life.

"Now go; I will help you speak and will teach you what to say."

Exodus 4:12

"Be on guard! Be alert! You do not know when that time will come."

Mark 13:33

"Opportunities present themselves every day — to everyone. You just have to be alert and ready to act."

Marc Ostrofsky
NYT Best Selling Author, Venture Capitalist, Entrepreneur

A Subway Ride in Beijing

On a cold and smoggy morning in January in Beijing, China, it was early and still very dark, with quite a chill in the air as I was walking from my friend's apartment in the northern part of Beijing out past the 5th ring highway to the subway station about a mile away. As I walked along quietly on the already crowded streets, among hundreds of other people on their way to work, my thoughts mostly centered on my family and how much I missed them since I'd been in China for the last two weeks. But I also turned my attention to the important business meeting I was traveling to in central Beijing that morning. I was meeting with a group of Chinese business owners to coach them on how to develop a successful and mature business.

After my 30-minute walk, I arrived at the subway station, which was bustling with people scurrying about in a hurry, filled with the unusual smells of street vendors selling food and the typical noises of a busy train station. As the train pulled into the station, it was so jam-packed with people that I was doubtful there would be room for me on board. The doors opened, and four people exited the train. Then like a wave hitting the beach, I was pushed onto the train along with about a dozen other people. The doors quickly closed, and we were underway. (Now I know what a sardine must feel like being put into the can!)

As the train pulled out of the station, a young woman standing several people away from me motioned in my direction and told me in English that the girl next to me was asking me in Mandarin if I was getting off at the next stop. Although I speak a little Mandarin, I did not realize that she was talking to me. I said no to her and stepped to the side so she could move closer to the doors.

After the next stop (and all of us sardines had been shuffled a bit), the young lady who had spoken to me in English was standing much closer to me. She was attractive and well dressed with a professional look. She addressed me again in English and said, "Good morning, how are you?"

As I usually do, in an attempt to make a good impression on any Chinese person I meet, I spoke to her in Mandarin: "Hen hao, zhao sheng hao, ni ne?" which means, "Good morning, I'm very well, and you?"

She asked if I lived in Beijing, and I said no but that I had traveled here several times for business. "Where are you from?" she said.

"I'm from the U.S. in the western part, Denver, Colorado."

What a Dilemma

Then after a few more pleasantries, I was totally amazed when she said to me, "I have a dilemma today. Maybe you can help me?"

Wow, what did she just ask me? How do you field a question like that? Even though it was early in the morning and the only reason I was fully awake was the cold walk to the subway station, I always try to be alert for the next divine appointment God has for me. So, I cautiously said to her that I would be glad to help if I could. And with that, I immediately lifted up a prayer in my mind: "Lord, what should I do with this young lady and her question? Please help me to represent You as Christ's Ambassador."

Her name was Julie and she explained to me that she worked as the administrative assistant for the CEO of a mining company headquartered in Beijing. The company is a joint venture with two Canadian and Chinese companies, and they mine coal in Mongolia. Then she explained her dilemma: She is responsible for the safe or lock box at work, where they keep petty cash and other important items. The previous day her key to the safe went missing for a while, and she was unsure about whether someone had stolen the key to make a copy or if she just misplaced it for a time. She didn't know if she should go to work this morning and confess what happened to her boss or if she should wait and hope that nothing bad happened. At any rate, she was quite concerned about what to do and fearful that she could get into big trouble at work and potentially lose her job.

"Lord, what should I do with this young lady and her question? Please help me to represent You as Christ's Ambassador."

My first thought was to tell her that "honesty is usually the best policy." But then she added that last year her boss, the CEO, was a Canadian businessman from Vancouver, and he was much kinder and more gracious that her new Chinese boss. She was very worried that he would not be understanding at all.

Unfortunately, my first thought was my only thought; that was all I had at the moment. So I said to her, "I believe that honesty is always the best approach, and I would be proactive in sharing with your boss exactly what happened and ask him to please help." I could tell immediately that she appreciated my comments but was really unsure about whether she should take my advice. And I was immediately thinking that I might have just gotten this nice, young lady fired from her job today.

So I quickly said to her that the decision about what to do really needed to be hers; she knew the situation better and should make her own decision. But in an effort to help her even more, I said, "Would it be OK if I pray for you about this today?" She replied that she was not much into religious things, and I reassured her that I would pray for her later today about her decision.

I took out my business card, which has English on one side and Chinese on the other side, and handed it to her. I did not ask for her contact information, lest she think I was a creepy old guy from America. I told her that I would really like to know what she decided and how it went, so I would really appreciate it if she would email me tonight. She nodded that she would and then thanked me for my help. My stop was coming up, so we exchanged goodbyes and "nice to meet you" and I was off to my meeting. As I headed through the subway station, my mind was spinning with what just unexpectantly happened in the last 20 minutes. But as I had promised her, I started praying for her as I walked through the subway station and down the street to my meeting, asking the Lord to help her with her decision at the office that morning.

Late that evening as I was working on my laptop at my friend's apartment, an email from Julie popped up. With great excitement and anticipation, I opened to read her news. *Hallelujah, it's good news!* She decided to take my advice and tell her boss what happened the day before. He was very kind and understanding and told her that he really appreciated her honesty and concern for the security of the company. He sent her out to get a brand-new safe to replace the current one. She was thrilled, as you can imagine. And for me, I breathed a big sigh of relief about the outcome.

Nothing Is Impossible with God

"Thank You, Lord, for this wonderful divine appointment today." We should be alert for divine appointments every day. "And thank You that I was alert enough and willing to engage with this young lady that You brought across my path this morning. I wonder how many other times You have brought people across my path and I've been too busy or preoccupied to recognize the opportunity You were giving me."

But there is far more to this story of God at work in our lives. Later that week I returned home to Denver and attended my first board meeting for a children's charity in Colorado. The informal meeting was held at the home of one of the other board members in a wealthy neighborhood. As we gathered around the island in the kitchen for drinks and hors d'oeuvres, Jessica, the founder of the organization, introduced me to Brad, the Chairman of the Board and a lawyer with a prestigious law firm in downtown Denver.

She said to Brad, "This is Victor I was telling you about. He does a lot of business in China." As we shook hands, Brad said that he had made a couple of trips to China in the last few years to do some legal work for a few clients. He said that the first trip he made about three years ago was to help a client in Denver in the LED lighting business set up a joint venture with a Hong Kong-based company that did manufacturing in Shenzhen. So I said to Brad, "Is that client by any chance Brad H. of XYZ Company here in Denver?"

With a rather puzzled look on his face, he said, "Yes, it is. How do you know them?"

I replied, "Well, my company, Summit Group International, had recently done some product sourcing work for them in China."

We should be alert for divine appointments every day.

OK, what a coincidence that must be, right? Then Brad said that he had also made two trips to Beijing to help a client in the mining business set up a joint venture with a Chinese company that mines coal in Mongolia.

I responded again to him, "Does that happen to be a mining company in Vancouver, Canada?"

Now Brad had moved from a puzzled look to a look of total shock and bewilderment. He cautiously said, "It is," and then stared at me like "How in the world could you know that?"

Well, guess what! The joint venture of the Chinese and Canadian coal mining companies was exactly the company that Julie, the young lady on the train, worked for. What are the odds of that happening? Now this was blowing my mind, too! When I told Brad and Jessica the rest of the story, they were totally dumbfounded. Of course, even as amazed as I was, I knew what had just happened. God was showing off! I picture Him laughing out loud as He watched the three of us trying to make sense of this one-in-a-billion connection.

I don't believe in coincidences. This was another divine appointment orchestrated by God to show His power and willingness to involve us in His plan to reconcile everyone to Himself. And while countless people have been confounded by this story, it was no big deal whatsoever for God to connect an American businessman halfway around the world and a young lady on a crowded subway in Beijing and a lawyer in Denver.

More Good (Great) News

But there is more to this story — and it's the best part. Over the next year, I stayed in touch with Julie through an occasional email here and there, asking about how she was doing and about her family just to get to know her better. I also shared some pictures and information about my family with her. Then as I prepared for another trip to Beijing, I emailed her to let her know when I would be there and suggested that maybe we could meet for coffee or lunch somewhere near her work. She agreed, and we set up a time and place at a coffee shop in a retail mall in downtown Beijing.

We had a wonderful visit and shared more about our lives, building a bond of trust and community. After about two hours of conversation, it was time for me to catch the train back to my hotel near the airport. But she had a personal car, which was quite unusual at that time for a young couple in China, and she offered to drive me to my hotel to save me time and the hassles of crowded subways and train stations and also for us to continue to visit. I have ridden in a number of cars driven by young people in China who have limited experience and training in operating a car, especially in the intense traffic conditions in a big city in China. But fortunately, Julie was a very good driver and did not give me any frightful experiences as we made the one-hour drive to my hotel.

It was really great to see her again and to realize that she trusted me enough to offer me a ride in her car. But the best part of the story is still to come.

Throughout this time after first meeting her on the subway, I had gently and respectfully shared a few comments about my faith in Jesus. And she seemed open to my thoughts. About six months after our coffee meeting in Beijing, she emailed me with an exciting message: Seven years earlier she had applied through the Chinese government for a lottery program that could result in getting a visa to move to Canada. She told me that she had really forgotten about it and assumed that it would not happen. But there it was — a visa for her to travel to Canada along with her nine-year-old daughter.

Now she faced another dilemma: The visa did not include her husband since they were not married when she first applied. She decided that she could not pass up this opportunity to make a better life for herself and her family — especially her daughter — so she accepted the visa to move to Canada without her husband. I can't imagine doing that myself, but I know how different her perspective must have been while growing up in China. The hope would be that her husband could join them in the future.

So I immediately connected her with a Chinese Christian friend of mine in Beijing, Jeffrey, who had attended college in Toronto and then worked for a large company there for several years before returning to China. He was able to help her with lots of information about living in Toronto and also made some contacts for her about finding a job there.

I also contacted my Chinese friend Richard, who had lived for many years in Toronto, and I asked for his help to find Julie a job and also to take her and her daughter to church.

As all of this was going on for several weeks prior to them coming to Toronto from Beijing, I talked with her on the phone briefly to see how she was doing. She said to me, "You are such a nice man, and I appreciate the things you're doing. But why are you doing all these things to help me?"

The answer to her question was similar to the one I gave Catherine in Nanjing: "It's because of my love of Jesus and what God has done for me. I wouldn't normally be this way, but He wants me to serve others."

A short few months later I received a text from her that she had accepted Jesus as her Savior, and she wanted to thank me for talking to her on the subway that morning and helping her to this point.

Hallelujah! Praise the Lord! Thank You, Father, for giving me the privilege to meet Julie and help lead her to You.

How often are we so caught up and absorbed in our own world that we miss out on opportunities to engage with other people — to "love God and love our neighbors"? It certainly would have been easy to do on a cold, snowy morning in Beijing on an overcrowded subway. Thankfully,

I was alert and willing to engage in the life of someone who God brought into my life.

My prayer is that you will also be more alert and willing to share the love and Gospel of Jesus Christ in your own life, ***As You Go***.

Living It Out, *As You Go*

Key Points to Remember

- You never know when God will arrange a divine appointment for you.
- Be alert to the people and situations around you at all times.
- Don't be too busy or preoccupied to respond when an opportunity presents itself. Make yourself available to God.

What Will I Do?

25. What would I do if I encountered someone like Julie in a public place?

____

____

____

26. What precautions and boundaries are necessary when sharing with someone of the opposite sex?

____

____

____

27. What is the importance of staying in touch to build a relationship and trust?

____

____

____

10

As You Go, Make Disciples!

Live your life enthusiastically and be willing to engage.

"Never be lacking in zeal, but keep your spiritual fervor, serving the Lord."

Romans 12:11

"It's faith in something and enthusiasm for something that makes a life worth living."

Oliver Wendell Holmes
Associate Justice of the Supreme Court of the United States

"Being engaged is a way of doing life, a way of living and loving. It's about going to extremes and expressing the bright hope that life offers us, a hope that makes us brave and expels darkness with light."

Bob Goff
NYT Bestselling Author of Love Does

I served on the Board of Directors of CBMC (Christian Business Men's Connection) International for four years. What a great experience and privilege it was to serve with a group of godly businesspeople from countries around the world. Near the end of my term, we had a two-and-a-half day board meeting prior to an All-Africa CBMC Conference. The event was held at a lake resort in the fairly remote location of Gariep Dam, South Africa, about a three-hour drive south of Bloemfontein and roughly halfway between Johannesburg and Cape Town. This trip to South Africa was my third in four years' time, and I was excited to see many friends and meet some new ones.

We stayed in modern cabins built around the lake and had our board meetings and meals at the Guest Center. So, for the first three days we ate all three meals each day at the restaurant at the Guest Center. The food was quite interesting, and one of my favorite dishes was the Meat Trio, which consisted of lamb, springbok (the South African version of a gazelle), and ostrich. The staff that served us were really friendly and provided top-notch service.

When the conference started, about 170 people from 9 countries in Africa and 5 other countries were in attendance. The meetings and events were held in a separate conference center, a short walk from the Guest Center. Dinners for the three nights of the conference were catered in the conference center. The last night was a special meal because they grilled various meats, sausages, and chicken on the barbie, which in South Africa is called having a "brai," the Afrikaans word for barbeque.

The board members continued to have breakfast and

lunch in the restaurant at the Guest Center. On the last day of the conference, I did not show up for breakfast that morning but stayed in my cabin to handle some business matters involving a couple of our suppliers in China.

A Lunch Date with Christ

When I finished, it was too early for lunch. But I decided that I would go ahead and take a leisurely walk up to the restaurant and read my devotional and write in my journal. No one was in the restaurant when I arrived, so I found a spot at one of the tables and spread out to read and journal. One of the nice ladies who seemed to be a supervisor or manager at the restaurant came over and asked if I wanted a drink.

When she returned with my glass of water and a soda, one of her co-workers was trailing along behind her. After setting the drinks down, she said, "May I ask you a question?" I replied, "Sure, what's up?"

She wanted to know if I remembered who was sitting at a certain table across the room at breakfast this morning. I told her that I did not make it for breakfast this morning; I had to stay in my cabin to get some work done.

Then she explained that there were three gentlemen sitting at the table this morning. As she was standing over by the entrance to the room, she noticed that they were praying together. She said, "I could feel their prayers, and they had a big impact on me and I started to cry." Her co-worker, Queen, who was now standing beside her, had walked up to her at that moment and said she could also feel their prayers.

So she said to me, "My name is Yolanda. Can you pray for me and my family?'"

I said, "I'd be glad to do that, but can we wait until everyone else comes for lunch and I can find out who are those three men praying this morning at breakfast." They agreed that waiting until after lunch would be fine.

When the rest of the group started arriving for lunch, I started asking people if they remembered who was sitting at that particular table this morning at breakfast. After making a few inquiries, somebody suggested that they thought it was Enrique Cepeda, Latin American Director for CBMC, and two other men. So when I saw Enrique, I went over to him and explained what this young lady had asked me before lunch.

Enrique said he would be glad to pray for them after lunch.

So, as some of the guys were finishing lunch and starting to leave, I waved to Yolanda and Queen to please come over to my table. And Enrique also headed over my way, followed by the other two men at the breakfast table, Edgar from Mexico City and Alex from Zambia. We then began to circle around these two ladies, along with a few other members of the CBMC group from several different countries there at lunch.

Before we could get started, three other ladies from the kitchen staff came out and joined the group. We all held hands, and Enrique asked Edgar if he would please say a prayer for these ladies in Spanish as he would translate into English. Edgar launched into a powerful prayer for these ladies and their families, pausing to let Enrique translate.

When he said "Amen," Enrique took charge and held hands with Yolanda. He said, "I believe God is doing something really special right here, right now. I'm going say a prayer and I want you to repeat the words back to me."

He prayed the sinner's prayer and they repeated it, and we all watched five ladies at this restaurant accept Jesus as their Lord and Savior. The ladies were crying; the rest of us were crying. It was a moment of great joy — all because God arranged a divine appointment and I said, "Yes, Lord."

We were smiling and crying and hugging and thanking and blessing, and gradually we started to disperse. Suddenly, two more ladies and two guys emerged from the kitchen area and basically asked if we could also pray for them. So we repeated the process with Edgar and Enrique, while circling around the four of them and holding hands. The outcome was the same! Four people prayed the sinner's prayer, and at the "amen," there were tears and joy and hugging by all.

Again, we started to disperse, shaking our heads in amazement at what we had just experienced. By the time we had almost reached the entrance to this section of the restaurant, two more young men came out of nowhere and asked the same question, "Would you please pray for us?" So we repeated the process again for the third time — with the same outcome.

At the "amen" this time, our minds were completely blown away. Everyone in this impromptu prayer team was overwhelmed, and I don't think any of us were able to keep our feet on the floor. We all curiously looked around the room and toward the entrance to see if by chance any more people were going to come out of the woodwork or drop from the ceiling to receive Jesus.

He prayed the sinner's prayer and they repeated it, and we all watched five ladies at this restaurant accept Jesus as their Lord and Savior.

No more people came, even though it would have been great if they had. Our group was giving high fives and hugs and just praising God for what we had the privilege to participate in — all for His honor and glory. In the short span of about 20 minutes, 11 South Africans had received Christ, and their lives and the lives of their family would never be the same. The sheer joy and excitement of being a part of this adventure was amazing and all because we were trying our best to be good, faithful, and alert Ambassadors for Christ, ***As We Go***.

Before I left, I noticed that Yolanda was standing over by the checkout counter, so I went over to greet her and tell her how wonderful it was to meet her. I asked her how I could continue to pray for her. She then shared that her husband was having lots of problems with alcohol and drugs, and it was hurting her and her two daughters terribly. He was being very abusive to the three of them, although Yolanda mentioned that he had not ever physically hurt them before. But she was afraid that it would get worse if he did not get help and stop hanging around with a bad group of guys.

At the "amen" this time, our minds were completely blown away.

A Wonderful New Friend

We exchanged contact information, primarily email addresses and phone numbers. As I departed, I gave her a big hug and told her I would be in touch again soon and would be continuing to pray for her, her husband, and her two girls.

With her permission, I was able to share this amazing story with the entire CBMC African Conference of about 200 people that following evening as a way to encourage everyone to be on the lookout for divine appointments from God. I also asked the group to please pray for Yolanda and her family, and I'm confident that many did and may still be praying.

I also spoke to Frik, Harm, and Ariana at the CBMC office in Cape Town, and they agreed to stay in touch with her, pray for her, and possibly have someone visit her if they were traveling near Gariep Dam. Ariana especially has emailed and called Yolanda and helped her in many ways on her journey.

As promised — and much to her surprise — I have been in contact with Yolanda many times in the last two years by email, text, and social media. I have learned more about her story, her husband, her two beautiful young girls, and her faith. I have been able to share pictures of my wife and children and grandchildren, including our three four-legged, furry girls.

Her husband had been doing better and was making some progress. But had still not changed into the husband and father he needs to be for his family. Unfortunately, a recent email from Yolanda sadly indicated that things had taken a turn for the worse. I'm confident that many in South Africa continue to pray every day for them. I would ask you to do the same and pray for God's blessing on Yolanda and her family. I know she will appreciate your love and support through prayer.

And I continue to pray for her and her husband almost every day, asking God for His help in transforming the heart and mind of her husband and protecting Yolanda and her two daughters. I also continue to thank God for what a blessing this story and this unusual relationship has been to me and to others I have told. And now I hope it will bless and encourage you as you seek to be a better Ambassador for Christ, ***As You Go***.

Living It Out, *As You Go*

Key Points to Remember

- Always be prepared to engage when someone asks you an important question.
- Be willing to share the Gospel anytime and anywhere with gentleness and respect.
- Continue to pray for the people that God has brought to you.

What Will I Do?

28. Do I see people the way Christ does, regardless of their job and station in life?

____

____

____

29. Am I willing to step out and take a chance when an opportunity arises like this?

____

____

____

30. How can I share the joy and love of Christ more often, ***As I Go***?

____

____

____

11

Relationships Matter!

God designed us to be in relationships!

"In your relationships with one another, have the same mindset as Christ Jesus."

Philippians 2:5

"Greater love has no one than this: to lay down one's life for one's friends."

John 15:13

"I don't like that man. I must get to know him better."

Abraham Lincoln
Former President of the United States

"Facts don't change our minds. Friendship does."

James Clear
Author, entrepreneur, and photographer

Over the years, people have always been interested in finding clever ways to share their faith, get people to church, and lead people to Christ without having to start an authentic relationship with someone.

The Gospel Blimp

One of the most hilarious approaches to this task was captured as a spoof on the church in the 1981 film "The Gospel Blimp."

Two of the main characters in the movie are George and Ethel, who are concerned about the salvation of their next-door neighbors but unsure how to reach them with the ***Good (Great) News*** of Jesus Christ. During an evening dinner at their home with several Christian couples, they begin to talk about how to reach the new neighbors. Their friend, Herm, hatches a crazy idea to use a blimp to proclaim the Christian message to the next-door neighbors and the other un-churched citizens of Middletown. The group forms a company, raises money to buy a used blimp, then commences to evangelize their hometown by towing Bible verse banners, dropping gospel tracts in people's yards, and broadcasting Christian music.

But as the plans get more outlandish, George and Ethel become increasingly uneasy about the approach of International Gospel Blimps Incorporated and its "Commander," Herm.

While their hearts were in the right place, their approach was simply ineffective. Finally, George and Ethel have had enough and decide to quit the group. But they still want to reach the Asian couple that had recently moved in next door. A couple of months later, George runs into "Commander" Herm at the hardware store. George reluctantly asks how the Gospel Blimp is doing, and Herm admits that there were so many problems that they had decided to disband the group. But then he says to George, "I saw the Asian couple that live next door to you at church last Sunday. Do you know how that happened?"

George explains that they heard from another neighbor that the man living next door was apparently sick with the flu. So he and Ethel decided to make a pot of homemade vegetable soup to take next door. They walked over to their neighbors and knocked on the door. Herm is astounded and interrupts: "Oh my, you actually walked over there and knocked on their door? What happened then?"

George tells Herm that a very nice woman opened the door, and he and Ethel introduced themselves as living next door. The lady was really kind and invited them into her house. Ethel gave her the soup and said she hoped that her husband would be feeling better, and hopefully they would get a chance to meet him soon. Then they walked back to their house, feeling happy about the good deed they had done and also having finally met the lady next door.

But Herm anxiously wants to know more: How did they end up coming to church? George explains that a couple of weeks later, they saw the man next door outside, and he walked over to say hello. He was feeling much better, so they invited him and his wife to come over to their house on the weekend to have a BBQ. The neighbors came, and we grilled some burgers and had a really nice time.

Now Herm is even more shocked: "You invited them

over to your house — unbelievable!"

This spoof on the church is hilarious but sad. God is less concerned about buildings and organizations than He is about relationships. Too often we have our focus in the wrong place.

Common Ground

I think God wants us to be engaging with our neighbors to develop relationships, to love one another, to find common ground, and to share the message of the Gospel with those who are unconvinced.

I believe that one of the inventions that Satan has used quite effectively against us is the garage door opener. We get in our car as the garage door goes up, we put the car in reverse to back out of the driveway, and then push the remote button in the car to close the garage door again. When we come home from work or from out running errands, we repeat the process and end up back in our house without having to stop and talk to anyone.

The garage door and the remote opening device are quite useful items. They're time-savers and excellent to keep you out of the rain and the snow. But they have become a great deterrent to neighbor relationships and community.

The sad truth is that a very high percentage of Americans do not know their four closest neighbors. Your next mission trip should be a walk to your next-door neighbor's house, ***As You Go***.

An important element in building meaningful relationships is Common Ground. You can almost always find something you have in common with another person. There is an endless list of items: children, grandchildren, profession, education, sports (you don't even have to like the same team to engage in a conversation), cars, pets, the love of BBQ ribs, what cleaners you use, the weather (obviously, if you're standing in your neighbor's yard, you have the weather in common), landscaping, hunting and fishing, and on and on.

Your next mission trip should be a walk to your next-door neighbor's house.

In the CBMC Living Proof Adventure videos, Sean McDowell makes the case about Common Ground beautifully: "It's amazing in our culture how we focus more on differences than similarities. I've found that with any human being on this planet, I have far more things in common than differences. We all want to have a job that's meaningful, we want relationships, we want to be accepted, and we want to have fun in life. And these are just human elements, and although we dress differently or come from a different place and talk differently and have different hobbies. But underneath all of that, are basic human needs that everybody shares. And I've found that it takes more work with some people than others, but if I'm willing to ask questions, if I'm willing to get out of my comfort zone and talk about things that are important to someone else, I always find that there's more common ground than I could have ever imagined."

I believe that listening — not speaking — is the most important skill in building relationships and sharing the Gospel.

But you do have to be intentional and spontaneous to engage with other human beings in the neighborhood, at work, or anywhere you go. Take your eyes and your thoughts off yourself and what you're doing, and notice someone else around you to start an engagement. You'll be amazed at the fun, interesting, fantastic relationships you will start building.

Can you ask another person an open-ended question and then listen? "Where are you from? What kind of work do you do? Do you have a family? Where did you go to school? What's your favorite sports team?" And then you can ask an even bigger and better question. "I'd like to learn more. Would you be willing to briefly tell me your story?"

Then shut up, pay close attention, and listen. Most people think that sharing the Gospel mostly involves speaking. I believe that listening — not speaking — is the most important skill in building relationships and sharing the Gospel. Remember: God gave us two ears and only one mouth, and it's not so we can listen in stereo.

Ask Good Questions

I happen to be writing this chapter while on vacation in Cabo San Lucas, Mexico. Early this morning, I got a cup of coffee and went down to the pool and hot tub overlooking the beach to enjoy this beautiful and peaceful setting. (And hopefully to do some more writing for this book!)

There was a couple in their 50s already in the hot tub. As it turns out, it was the man's 50th birthday today. How did I find that out? I asked a few questions and listened.

The conversation started with the usual: "Where are you from?" The answer was Seattle. "Is this your first time to Cabo?" "What do you like most about coming here?" "What kind of business are you involved in?" "Interesting, tell me more about that."

"Would you be willing to briefly tell me your story?"

Before you know it, we'd been talking non-stop for 30 to 45 minutes and getting to know a lot about each other. They were very nice people, and we found a lot of common ground. I even got to share part of my story, letting them get to know me and hopefully developing a trusting relationship. I mentioned that I might be coming to Seattle in the next couple of months on business and maybe we could meet for coffee. "Absolutely!" they said. So we exchanged contact information. They were flying back to Seattle that day, so I simply said, "Nice meeting you. Have safe travels and hope to see you again in a few months."

Wow, that was exhausting, I need a nap. Are you kidding me? It was a great joy and pleasure to meet this nice couple and share some things about our lives while sitting in a hot tub overlooking the beach and the Sea of Cortez. Did you catch the sarcasm?

I never cease to be amazed at how private and isolated so many people are in this world. We've lost the ability to engage with people and build relationships, whether it's our next-door neighbors or a couple from Seattle in the hot tub in Cabo. Will I ever see this couple again? I have no idea. But

I am asking God what he wants me to do with the beginnings of a relationship after this 45-minute encounter. It may be nothing more than the three of us enjoying a fun conversation to start our day. Or it may be much more than that, like having the opportunity to lead them to Christ or make a lifetime friendship.

The next day in the early morning in the same hot tub in Cabo, I met a couple from Portland, Oregon. They were originally from Romania but had been living in the U.S. for 30 years. We had a similar nice conversation, but nothing more. The day after that, I ran into them near their condo, and we said hello again. On the third day, I followed my same routine of coffee and the hot tub in the morning, and you'll never guess who was there: my new best friends from Portland, of course.

Sometimes I don't always get it the first time, but God is persistent with me, and generally I get it by the third time. This morning David was reading a book by a Christian author. So I asked him about it, and we started a conversation. I told him that I was writing a book about Matthew 28:19. He said he'd like to get a copy when it was published. Then he added, "You know, I was thinking that I should share more with a couple we met in the hot tub before you arrived this morning, but for some reason I didn't. I need to be more open about sharing."

We exchanged contact information, and hopefully we will see each other again next year. They have a niece living in Denver, and they plan to visit. And I may have a business trip to Portland. Amazing how God works if you're paying attention!

About three years ago, almost the exact same encounter happened at the pool at The Bay Club at Waikoloa Beach Resort on the Big Island in Hawaii. My wife and I struck up a conversation with a couple about our same age from Houston, Texas. It turned into a great match. We've been to see them in Houston, they will probably come to visit us in Colorado, we have talked about going on vacation to Hawaii together in the future, and there is no doubt in my mind that we will have a great relationship with Joan and Mark for the rest of our lives.

It seems to me that I need to be spending more time at the pool and the beach to make some great friends! You can do the same thing whenever and wherever you are, ***As You Go***.

Living It Out, *As You Go*

Key Points to Remember

- Your next mission trip should be a walk to your next-door neighbor's house.
- Listening — not speaking — is the most important skill in building relationships and sharing the Gospel.
- Facts don't change our minds; friendship does. Relationships really matter.
- An important element in building meaningful relationships is Common Ground.

What Will I Do?

31. If I don't already know my four closest neighbors, what can I do to change that?

    ____

    ____

    ____

32. What do I have in common with my neighbors? Make a list.

    ____

    ____

    ____

33. What can I do to become a more effective listener?

    ____

    ____

    ____

12

Gentleness and Respect!

God Saves, Not You. Loosen up and have fun.

"But in your hearts revere Christ as Lord. Always be prepared to give an answer to everyone who asks you to give a reason for the hope that is in you. But do this with gentleness and respect."

1 Peter 3:15

"Treat what you love with gentle kindness and appreciative respect."

J. Kevin Earp
Author

Enrique Cepeda, a dear friend of mine and the Latin American Director for CBMC International, has more fun being an Ambassador for Christ than anyone I have ever known. He is so positive, energetic, and fun-loving every time I have ever seen him. He is now in his late 70s and going strong. Talk about finishing well: That would be Enrique.

Even though I am happy to be a member of the Enrique Cepeda Admiration Society, he is always quick to tell anyone that it's not about him — but all about Jesus. He always gives the thanks and praise to God for anything he can do to further God's Kingdom here on earth. He feels honored and blessed that God has given him the privilege and the heart for being His Ambassador.

He has hundreds of stories about meeting people and sharing the Gospel, ***As He Goes***. He should probably write a book himself filled with these stories so everyone can see how easy and fun it can be to share Christ in a hurting, secular world.

The Friendly Skies

One of my favorite stories about Enrique is the time he was in the middle seat in economy on a two-hour flight back home to Oklahoma City. Are you beginning to see a pattern here? You have to get out of the house and maybe even travel somewhere for God to arrange these divine appointments, ***As You Go***.

During the roughly three million miles that I have flown on an airplane in my life, I have had many occasions where the person sitting next to me immediately pulled out their headset, did not make eye contact with me, and did every other imaginable thing to communicate to me that they have no interest in talking with me, "so please leave me alone." I can somewhat understand that at times you just need some down time to rest or sleep or watch a movie on a long flight. But if I'm going to be sitting, eating, and sleeping eight inches away from someone for the next 3 or 7 or 14 hours, shouldn't we at least exchange pleasantries and our names and maybe have a little further conversation?

But as you probably know if you've flown at all, the experience generally involves some small talk. "Where are you from? Where are you going? What do you do?" (This last question has always puzzled me. What do I do about what? Of course, the question is always meant to be about your work or business or vocation.)

So, as Enrique settled into his seat, he engaged the man next to him in the aisle seat in his typical gregarious manner. The first part of the conversation from Enrique was no doubt friendly, fun loving, and energizing. The man quickly became interested and was enjoying the conversation with my friend.

Then came time for the inevitable big question. "What do you do?" Enrique asked the man. He replied, "I'm an insurance agent." Enrique quickly came back with, "Me, too. I'm also in the insurance business."

The man then said, "My father is the owner of the company." Enrique said, "My Father is also the owner of our business. What kind of insurance do you offer?"

The man said, "The best product we have is life insurance because it is the least expensive in the nation." Enrique replied, "I also offer life insurance, but it is a much different kind of life insurance than you offer."

"Oh, really. What do you mean?" the man said.

"Well, in order for the person to receive any benefit from your insurance, they have to pay and pay and pay every year until they die. And then, of course, they don't get to enjoy the benefit because they're dead. It's really more like death insurance than life insurance. The insurance I offer gives you an immediate benefit as soon as you sign up and even carries forward after you die."

By now, the businessman was beginning to think, "Who is this character or even crazy person sitting next to me for the next two hours? He's probably trying to sell some bizarre scheme to unsuspecting people in order to make money."

Enrique continued, "And this life insurance I offer will not cost you anything, yet it will cost you everything. And then you get to enjoy it even more after you die."

After those last statements, the man in the seat next to Enrique is sure he's listening to a scam or a clever joke, and he can't wait for the punchline. So he finally says, "Please tell me more about your life insurance."

You're probably catching on to where this is going.

With gentleness and respect, Enrique shares the free gift of eternal life from God through His Son, Jesus Christ. He simply and kindly shares the ***Good (Great) News***.

After some questions and further discussion for about 30 minutes, the insurance salesman decides that he wants the kind of life insurance that Enrique is representing and prays the sinner's prayer at 30,000 feet to accept Jesus as his Lord and Savior.

What a beautiful story and wonderful outcome! Enrique was just flying home on a plane, and God made a divine appointment for him to sit next to this man and share the Gospel. And he did it in a fun and relaxed way, realizing all the time that this man's salvation was in God's hands, and the heart of this man was not his own responsibility. Enrique was just playing the part he was asked to play at that moment and place in time.

It's quite possible that the man could have rejected the message Enrique shared with him. That would have been OK, even though God wants all His children to come to know Him. You must remember that this conversation may have just started the man thinking about the eternal destiny of his soul, and someone else might come along later to reap the harvest. And that process might have taken many more years and many more encounters with the message of Christ.

But Enrique can feel wonderful about what he did that day by being obedient to what God put in front of him and to the command of Christ in the Great Commission to "go and make disciples of all nations," ***As You Go***.

A Birthday Surprise

This book was already written and in the editing phase when I got an email early in the morning, as I was on the shuttle bus at the airport in Denver to catch a flight. The message brought tears to my eyes. After walking into the terminal, I texted Nan to see if she was awake, and she called me back. I shared the back story of the email with her and wept as I read the message. When I finished, she said, "This story must be in the book"! And I agreed. So here it is.

About six years before this email, my product sourcing company, Summit Group International, had chosen a Hong Kong-based company with a factory in Shenzhen, China, to print high-end shopping bags for a famous retail brand. I had visited the factory with my team and had met the General Manager along with the key staff. We reviewed their operations and talked about this new business. The first order looked great and was completed on time.

The owner of the company, Jimmy, is headquartered in Hong Kong and could not be at the factory for our visit, but he called to express his regrets. I was going to be in Hong Kong later that week, so we agreed to meet at the airport one morning before my flight.

Somehow I had learned that it was Jimmy's birthday, likely from someone at the factory. So I decided to get him a birthday cake with a nice note and bring it to our first meeting. He was overwhelmed by this gesture of friendship, and we began what would turn out to be a great business and personal relationship.

After thanking me profusely for the cake, Jimmy commented that it was really the people at the factory who deserved the cake for their good work. I replied, "Well, maybe I should get one for them." He chuckled and said that would be nice but really not necessary.

We moved on to share about our business, family, and a few other interesting topics to get to know each other better. I vaguely remember "raising the flag" by saying something about God or my faith. He asked if I was a Christian, and I proudly confirmed I was. I can't remember my exact questions back to him, but I do remember coming away from the meeting suspecting that Jimmy knew about God but likely did not have a personal relationship with Christ.

Between our meeting and my flight back to the U.S., I instructed the Sourcing and Quality Control Manager for my company, whose English first name is also Jimmy, to get a cake and take it to the factory in China early the following week. He ended up buying cupcakes and taking them to the roughly 60 employees at the printing factory. The general manager and the workers were amazed and very pleased that their efforts had been recognized, even in a simple but uncommon way. The owner in Hong Kong, Jimmy, sent me an immediate email and expressed how amazed he was by this gesture of appreciation and care for him and his people.

Over the last six years we have done business together successfully and developed an even more trusting and serving relationship.

As I was finishing this book, I sent a wire transfer for $50,202 to Jimmy in Hong Kong for the balance payment on a recent order. Unfortunately, my bank has a limit of $50,000 per transfer per day, so the transfer was $202 short. Jimmy emailed me the next day and notified me of the situation. I checked and realized what had happened to the wire transfer and informed him that I would send the balance of $202 immediately the next day.

He replied with the following email:

> Victor,
>
> Thanks for clarify. Do you mind doing me a

> favor? I know a good man who has a wonderful granddaughter, Lia, going to 4 years old on March 29. Would you please help me to use this $202 to buy her a birthday cake? I beg you to pay the extra if this small amount is not enough. Please don't mention to others that this cake is coming from me, but from her Great grandfather who gave something like 5 Loaves & 2 Fish to others.
>
> I also want to take this opportunity to THANK YOU for all you have done for us through the years. May God's face smile on you and your family always.
>
> Sent with Love and gratitude that you have been in my life.
>
> Jimmy K.

And you can now see why it brought tears of great joy to me and my family. Thank you so much, Jimmy!

(P.S. – We ordered a custom cake for Lia, and it was a big hit at the party!)

With Respect

Remember that the scripture in 1 Peter 3:15 says to "do this with gentleness and respect." This approach is where so many believers misunderstand or even misrepresent what God wants them to do in sharing their faith with the unconvinced.

For some reason, many people think that the first step in reaching an unbeliever is to convince them of their sin through being judgmental and self-righteous. I have found that most people already know they are not living a perfectly holy, righteous life and don't need you to point that out to them in an offensive way.

What the unbeliever wants is someone who approaches it in a completely different manner than what they expect. Out of sincere love, not judgement. Out of respect, not disrespect. And out of kindness and caring, not condemnation.

And 1 Peter 3:15 also says to "be prepared to give a reason for the hope that is in you." By being prepared, does that mean having your Master of Divinity from seminary and having the Bible memorized? Quite the contrary: It just means to be on the lookout, be alert, and watch for opportunities. And when God brings someone across your path, then relax, pray about what He wants you to do, start a conversation, be led by the Holy Spirit (God will give you the thoughts and words to say), have fun, and make a new friend.

If the opportunity arises, share something about your faith. If there's more of an opening or the other person asks a question, give them more information about the Gospel message.

And if you somehow screw it up and don't say the right thing, it's OK. Try again and again, and God will show you what to do and say. But please don't think of a "But" why you can't do it — because you truly can.

Just love God, show up, hang loose, and have fun. You might just end up making a new friend for life. Or you might just have someone join you in heaven for eternity. But most of all, be obedient to Christ's two Great Commandments — love God and love your neighbor, and go and make disciples of all nations, ***As You Go***.

Living It Out, *As You Go*

Key Points to Remember

- Think about clever and fun ways to connect with people and open their hearts and minds to hear the Gospel.
- Be prepared to give an answer for the hope that is in you with gentleness and respect.
- Remember that a person's salvation is between God and that person; it's not your responsibility.
- Just love God, show up, hang loose, and have fun.

What Will I Do?

34. What can I do to avoid making someone feel judged and condemned?

____

____

____

35. What changes can I make to show more of Christ's love in all my relationships?

____

____

____

36. How can I display more gentle kindness and appreciative respect to everyone around me?

____

____

____

13

Stories Are Interesting, Yours and Mine

Would you share your story with me?

"Let the redeemed of the LORD tell their story — those he redeemed from the hand of the foe, those he gathered from the lands, from east and west, from north and south."

Psalm 107:2-3

"There is something in us, as storytellers and as listeners to stories, that demands the redemptive act, that demands that what falls at least be offered the chance to be restored."

Flannery O'Connor
American novelist and short story writer

The month of October was extremely busy with travels for me. As I mentioned in Chapter 11, I had spent a week in Johannesburg, South Africa, with friends and then another week in Gariep Dam, attending a CBMC International Board Meeting and an All-Africa Conference with Christians from 14 countries. My cup was already overflowing after all the wonderful people and experiences in South Africa. I was home for 36 hours to reload my luggage, and then Nan and I flew to Jacksonville, Florida, to attend a CBMC USA Board Meeting and President's Council event with staff and donors on nearby Amelia Island.

My energy tank was running on fumes, and several people expressed their concerns about how exhausted I looked and asked if my health was OK. I was also concerned that I looked drained enough that people were commenting about it, and I was hoping it was just the travels and not my heart again.

After a week of work and meetings and dinners in Florida, we flew to Houston to spend a few days, hopefully resting, to visit our dear friends Kay and Zeke. We stayed at a Marriott Courtyard hotel in The Woodlands near where they live so we could get some rest.

Selling Muffins and Sharing God's Love

About 8 a.m. on Saturday morning I went down to the hotel lobby to order some coffee and a muffin, and there behind the counter was Julia, an attractive black woman in her 60s.

I had brought a file folder and a well-worn copy of a devotional book called *Jesus Calling* by Sarah Young. After

I ordered, Julia said, "Sir, could you turn that book over?" When she saw the front cover, she said, "I love that book! Is this a new version?"

I replied, "No, I have had this one for about six years and have been writing in it almost every day." She told me that she had Version 2 and had heard that the original version was really great. But unfortunately, she had not been able to find one.

I was wearing one of my "AsYouGo" t-shirts with the Last/First design printed on the front. I asked her what she thought about it, and she looked at it intently for a few seconds. Then with a big smile she said, "God's Word tells us that the First will be Last and the Last will be First. Oh, my goodness!"

So I showed her some of the pictures on my phone of the other t-shirt designs that we had created to help believers share their faith. She really liked the one with the hearts — "God made all the hearts the same," she said.

As I thanked her and started to walk away with my coffee and muffin to have some quiet time sitting in the lobby, Julia said to me, "Let me know if God gives you a word for me."

"Absolutely," I said.

So I sat in a comfy chair in the lobby with my coffee and muffin and started to read the daily devotional in *Jesus Calling*. Then I prayed and thanked the Lord for meeting Julia that morning and for her love for Him. "Lord, do You have any words for Julia this morning?" He quickly brought two thoughts clearly into my mind. The first had to do with the role of the Holy Spirit in prayer. When I was at the African conference in South Africa two weeks earlier, I led a discussion on this subject during the 6 a.m. to 7 a.m. prayer time, where about half of the 170 attendees to the conference showed up that early in the morning. One of my comments had to do with how many believers feel like they are praying to God who is far off in heaven or somewhere in the Cosmos. But in fact, if you have accepted Christ as your personal Savior, then we are actually praying to Him right inside of yourself and myself.

She really liked the one with the hearts — "God made all the hearts the same," she said.

The second thought the Lord gave me was how very encouraging Julia had been to me that morning, especially about the new "AsYouGo" venture.

I finished my quiet time and prayers a short time later and noticed that Julia was quite busy helping the other hotel guests with breakfast and coffee. I thought it was best to wait until she was not so busy before I went back up to share these thoughts with her.

In the meantime, as I sat there checking a few messages on my cell phone, I noticed two women go up to the counter to talk with Julia for a couple of minutes. And Julia then came walking around from behind the counter and gave both of these ladies a big hug, laughed and smiled with them, and then wished them well and "God bless."

How about that! Now besides the two thoughts God had given me to share with her, I had one of my own.

When I noticed there was a lull in activity at the counter, I went up and told her that I had three thoughts to share with her — two from God and one from me. She was very pleased to hear those first two thoughts. Then I shared with her my thought: "While you may think that you are here mostly to dispense coffee and muffins, what you're doing here is dispensing love to everyone, the love of Christ flowing through you to so many. And what a blessing that is!"

How many of us could do 1,000 times more loving others, like Julia? I know I could. And I hope and pray that this simple, yet profound encounter will touch your life, like it did mine, and help us to open the doors to our hearts to pour out the inexhaustible love of Christ in us.

As if that morning's experience had not already been enough for me to not need an airplane to fly back home to Denver, there was still another powerful God moment about to happen. Julia thanked me for sharing those thoughts with her, and then she added, "When you first walked away with your coffee and muffin after showing me the pictures of the 'AsYouGo' t-shirts, I turned to walk back into the kitchen, and the Lord spoke to me. He said, 'This is going to be so much more than you can even think or imagine. It will spread everywhere because so many people need to know Me.'"

Oh, my! I was hoping that God wanted to use "As You Go" in a powerful way, but no one had ever verbalized that to me before Julia did. Do you know that feeling when something amazing and unexpected has happened and you are stunned and excited to the point of exploding? That's how I felt, and I walked down the hall to my room with tears of joy rolling down my face after my divine encounter with Julia.

How many of us could do 1,000 times more loving others, like Julia?

Later that day, I searched online to see if I could find one of the original versions of the *Jesus Calling* devotional book, and I found one on an obscure website that carried used Christian books. I ordered it and had it sent to Julia's home address in Houston. Then I sent her a handwritten note to tell her it was on the way and to thank her for the love and kindness that she had shown me on that Saturday morning.

I have not been in touch with her recently, but I hope to meet up with her again soon on another visit to Houston. You can be sure of one thing: Wherever she is, she is doling out large portions of Christ's love and joy and kindness to whoever she meets, ***As She Goes***! God bless you, Julia!

Share Stories

We all have stories that God has given us about our lives. Some are more dramatic and tragic or amazing and inspirational than others. And while we all love to be inspired by a powerful story, most of us cannot relate to those larger-than-life stories. We can generally relate much better to the normal, average, everyday stories of what happened in your life, because that's most often what's happening in the other person's life.

Stories about kids and marriage and work and sports and travels and health, stories that show how God was at work in your life and how you handled it. If you are a drug addict or an alcoholic or a victim of abuse, you may benefit greatly from a story of struggle and restoration through such horrible trials and situations. Fortunately, the vast majority of us have not had to deal with such challenging issues. But everyone is dealing with other typical life issues everyday, and when you are willing to share that story and include your faith in Christ as the most important part of the story, you can give friends, family, co-workers, and even strangers hope about their future. And maybe they will even see the ultimate answer to their life — the eternal, saving grace of Jesus.

We all have stories that God has given us about our lives.

So, can you share a story or two about how God has worked in your life? It's quite easy because we are all telling stories about what happened in our lives. We just need to include Jesus in those stories.

One mistake that a lot of people (me included) make when talking with others is talking too much, making the conversation all about us. And you may have some great things to share. But the best approach is to ask the other person powerful, open-ended questions and get them telling you about their life. A simple question for someone you just met or don't know very well is to say, "I would really enjoy hearing your story. Would you be willing to share some of it with me?" I've never had anyone say no. And then shut up and listen, keep listening, and pay attention.

Then and only then, if they ask you a question or want you to share your own story, is it appropriate to start sharing. Ideally, in these types of conversations you should listen about 80% of the time and talk 20%. They will walk away amazed and pleased that you showed so much interest in them and their story. You made them feel important and like you cared about them. When that happens, people are much more likely to be willing to listen to what you have to say.

You've probably heard the saying that "people don't care how much you know, until they know how much you care." And it's so true! And it's so simple! It's sharing the love of Christ and taking our eyes off ourselves. For a sometimes self-centered only child, that's hard for me to do.

Ideally, in these types of conversations you should listen about 80% of the time and talk 20%.

But think about all the stories in the New Testament about the interactions that Jesus had with all kinds of people. He gave us the model for human engagement. He asked powerful, open-ended questions. He answered a question with His own question. He listened intently before He spoke. When He did speak, it was with truth in love. He showed how much He cared about each individual — no matter their circumstances or station in life.

Isn't that what Christ is calling us to do in order to love people everywhere and to share the ***Good (Great) News***? Isn't that what He is calling us to do as His Ambassadors in the world. Isn't that what He is commanding us to do when He said, "Therefore, go and make disciples of all nations"?

I believe the answer is an emphatic "Yes." Then let's do it — starting now — ***As You Go***!

Living It Out, *As You Go*

Key Points to Remember

- Be willing to ask the question, "Would you share your story with me"?
- We all have stories that God has given us about our lives.
- We should listen about 80% of the time and talk 20%.
- Jesus gave us the model for human engagement.

What Will I Do?

37. What stories has God given me? How about writing them down and thinking about how I can use them?

____

____

____

38. How can I discipline myself to talk less and listen more?

____

____

____

39. How can I show people that I care more about what they think and say?

____

____

____

14

Invitations May Be All You Need!

Meet, greet, and invite — it can be that simple.

"For many are invited, but few are chosen."

Matthew 22:14

"Uplifting greetings bring a better spirit to your relationship."

Brent M. Jones
Author of Simply the Best

"True agape love can be defined as 'the steadfast, sacrificial zeal that diligently, objectively, seeks the true good of another.'"

Del Tackett
Former president of Focus on the Family Institute, creator of The Truth Project and the film, Is Genesis History?

Nan and I have 3 cute, little fur-babies at home that have been part of the family for over 10 years. Truthfully, they are nicer than some of our family — a lot nicer. If any of my family is reading this book, you know who you are. The girls are a dachshund named Maddy, a Chiweenie named Emma, and a Yorkshire Terrier named Lily. Emma and Lily are both rescues. Actually, they love me more unconditionally than any living thing on the planet. Just sayin'...

God Can Use a Chiweenie Named Emma

Earlier this year, I took the girls outside for a short walk. When I came back in the front door to our townhouse, I was taking off their leashes as they danced around before we headed up the stairs. Apparently, I did not pull the door completely shut and lock it.

A short time later that Friday afternoon in the summer, I knocked off work a little early and walked over to the pool by going down the stairs in the back and out the garage. When I returned about 45 minutes later, Maddy and Lily greeted me with their usual excitement, but Emma was nowhere to be found. I called her and looked all over the house, hoping she had simply gotten stuck in the closet or something.

Then I looked down the front stairs, and to my horror, the front door was standing ajar. I ran down into the yard and started calling for her, but I couldn't find her. I ran back to the house and started driving around our huge complex and park, frantically looking for her. But nothing!

Since I had been gone for at least 45 minutes, she could

have left quite a while before I got back home to discover her missing. She could have gone far away. She could have gotten to the main street, which is not too far from the house, and gotten run over by a car. The coyotes could have eaten her.

Needless to say for my pet-loving friends, I was devastated that I had lost one of my babies and that I was to blame for her getting out the front door. A dear friend, Mike Voelkelt, who loves my dachshunds almost as much as I do, came over to help scour the neighborhood until it got dark.

It was a long, sad night with lots of tears and very little sleep. I felt so helpless and was grieving this loss. Since I believe that God knows everything, I prayed without ceasing that He would protect Emma and bring her back to me. He knew all along where she was.

When it was light outside the next morning, I went to my computer and made a flyer with Emma's picture and my contact information. Then I went around the complex to all the central mailbox locations and posted the flyer in hopes that someone had seen her. Then I waited and waited and waited, but there were no calls. By about 3 p.m. that afternoon I was dealing with the realization that she was gone, and I would never see her again.

Then suddenly I got a phone call from an unknown number, so I didn't answer it. Immediately after that, a text came through that said, "I found your dog." OMG! OMG! OMG! I burst into tears of joy and started yelling for Nan to share the news. For some of you who have never known the unconditional love of a dog, I'm sorry you don't get it; you've truly missed out on a lot. But for me, it was really like a family member had been brought back from the dead.

Emma is a cheerful and friendly little girl; she has never met a stranger without wanting to lick their face. So, when she got out of the house, she turned right and wandered around the corner to the third townhouse to the left of us. A young couple in their early 30s, who we had seen and briefly said hello to in passing, lived there with their 5-year-old daughter. From their accent we suspected that they were from Russia. Emma wandered over to their patio where the little girl, Elizabeth, was playing and just invited herself to play and followed her into the house.

Her father, Ivan, had called the management office for the complex to report this lost dog. But they had not yet received any word of a lost dog, so he did not know what to do next except take care of her. By the time I thought about stopping by the office to see if anyone had reported a missing dog, the office was closed for the day.

I immediately went over to Ivan's house and had a great reunion with my precious, little girl, Emma. I thanked them and thanked them over and over again for taking care of my baby. I was so relieved and excited to have Emma back. Thank You, Lord.

Let's Meet for Coffee

Well, I hope you've enjoyed this story, but the best is yet to come. A few days later as I was driving by, Ivan walked out of his townhouse that exact moment. I slowed down to wave and say hello. The Holy Spirit prompted me to invite him for coffee. So I said, "By the way, do you by any chance work from home?"

He said, "Yes, I do."

"So do I," I replied. "How about going to meet for coffee later this week if you're available? I can stop by and pick you up."

Ivan answered, "Great, I would like that."

If you've read this far in this book, most of you can imagine where this story is headed. We had a two-and-a-half hour conversation at the coffee shop nearby. It turns out that he and his wife, Diana, are originally from the Ukraine and have been in the U.S. about six years. He works in IT and does special development projects with a firm in Dallas.

Early in our conversation, I asked him simply if he would tell me more about his story. Over an hour later, he took a breath and asked me about my story. We had a great time talking and sharing and laughing and starting a new personal relationship.

As we headed back home in the car, Ivan said that he really liked to search for and learn the truth about life. I told him that I had given a lot of thought to the meaning and purpose of life, and since I was further down the road than he was, maybe we could meet again for coffee soon and talk more about it. He thought that was a great idea!

We met again the next week and just spent more enjoyable time getting to know each other and our stories better. As we were driving back home this time, I said, "We didn't really get around to talking about the meaning of life today. How about I email you some information and we can discuss more next time we meet?" He agreed and we setup another coffee meeting in two weeks.

When we met the third time, we finally got around to talking more about the meaning of life. Ivan had looked at the first part of the information that I sent him, so he began to realize where I was coming from. Early in this conversation he said to me, "I know you are a Christian, and I need to let you know that I may tell you some things that will cause you to question your beliefs."

"That's fine," I responded, "as long as you realize that I may say some things that will cause you to question what you believe."

Ivan then said, "Every time I tell a Christian that, they are usually finished and don't want to talk to me anymore. They don't want to listen to me and hear what I think. If I can't quickly switch my beliefs, then they are done with me."

"Well, that's not me," I told him. "I'm very interested in what you think and why you believe what you believe. I don't think I have ever met anyone who has read and studied more about all the major religions."

"Well, OK then," he said. "Let's keep meeting and talking."

Simple Questions

The key element in our conversations is not for me to talk and explain everything about Christianity, trying to make a compelling argument to get him to adopt that point of view. No, the best way to continue reaching out to him is to ask powerful open-ended questions and then listen. This model is exactly the one often used by Jesus. He asked a lot of questions. Many times, He would answer a question with a question. Then after He listened to their response, He would often ask another question or maybe several more. Finally, He might respond with a great answer.

Just as in the story about the business group in South Africa, I have been dumbfounded to see how many people have difficulty asking even simple questions and building a relationship with a stranger, especially if it might lead to eventually sharing the Gospel. Since I grew up as a child being very shy, I can relate to this hesitancy. But in many cases, I've seen successful business and professional people — even people involved in sales and marketing — not be able to pull this trigger to start a relationship like this.

I don't want to insult anybody's intelligence, but maybe it would help if I could offer a few suggestions about what to say when you meet, greet, and invite:

- I really like that jacket. Where did you get it?
- Do you come here often? How's the service?
- Can I pet your dog? I've got three of them at home!

There are a thousand and one things that will start a conversation. Keep in mind that you're looking for common ground.

Then you can introduce yourself and ask some of the standard questions that often happen on an airplane:

- What do you do? (That's shorthand for asking what kind of work you do or business you're in)
- Where do you live? Where are you originally from?
- I'm interested in knowing more. Would you briefly share your story with me?

And then if this conversation seems to be going somewhere and you are getting the sense through the Holy Spirit that God wants you to take the next step, you can make an invitation:

- I'd like to learn more about your business (or whatever it may be). Would you be open to meeting for coffee in the next couple of weeks?
- Would you be interested in playing golf together sometime soon?
- I would love for you to meet my wife. Would you and your wife like to come over to our house this weekend? We're having a few neighborhood couples over for a BBQ.

See how easy it can be. If you're not good at this, it just takes a few suggestions like these and a little practice. And what's the worst thing that can happen? The stranger that you've never met before and may likely not ever see again will not be interested in having coffee with you or getting to know you better, so they'll say "thanks but no thanks." And off you'll both go, without any bruises or brain damage, to the next interaction with a human being. You can also silently pray, "Well, God, I guess that wasn't someone You wanted me to connect with."

Do I know where this is going with Ivan and what God wants me to do? No, not really. Do I think that God orchestrated me leaving the front door ajar, so Emma could get out and go to Ivan's house? Yes, I do. Do I know the outcome of this new relationship, in other words, if he will accept Christ and change his life for eternity? No, I don't.

But one thing is for sure: I have met a new friend who is very interesting and enjoyable to be with. I pray for him almost every day in my quiet time in the morning. Whatever happens regarding Ivan's salvation is in God's hands and Ivan's heart, and I'm doing my best to be faithful to the process.

Stay tuned — God is at work and He is giving me the great privilege of being a part of that work. He will give you the same privilege if you are willing to be engaged, **As You Go**.

A few months after meeting Ivan and during the final editing on this book, my precious Emma died suddenly from a stroke at the age of 11. So sad, but so blessed to have had her in our lives for 11 years.

Living It Out, *As You Go*

Key Points to Remember

- Often you can simply ask a person if they will tell you more about their story.
- The best way to reach out to someone is to ask powerful open-ended questions and then listen.
- God is at work and He is giving you the privilege of being a part of that work.

What Will I Do?

40. How can I learn to ask more and better open-ended questions?

    ____

    ____

    ____

41. If I tend to dominate conversations, what can I do to change that behavior?

    ____

    ____

    ____

42. Am I willing to be more outgoing and initiate conversations while asking God what He wants me to do?

    ____

    ____

    ____

15

Stay in Touch and Keep Praying!

It's in God's time, not yours.

"For God says, 'At just the right time, I heard you. On the day of salvation, I helped you.' Indeed, the 'right time' is now. Today is the day of salvation."

2 Corinthians 6:2

"With God, there's always an appointed time for things, and when you put Him first, trust in His timing, and keep the faith, miracles happen!"

Germany Kent
American Journalist and Author

Great Life Lesson

I want to start this chapter with one of the most important lessons I've ever learned about human relations.

Over a decade ago, before I started my own company, I lived and worked in Shanghai for a U.S. company for about four months to work with new factories and set up a warehouse/fulfillment center. The experience was phenomenal, and I wouldn't trade it for anything. But it was definitely the most challenging and satisfying experience of my business career.

Shanghai is a great city, and I truly enjoyed spending time there and experiencing the many things it has to offer. I was really blessed to get to know about 70 employees that we hired at the fulfillment center. I also had started learning to speak Mandarin, which must be one of the hardest languages to learn on the planet. So I got a lot of practice at work, in taxis, while shopping in the grocery store, at restaurants, and everywhere else. I will probably not master it or even speak it reasonably well in my lifetime here on earth. But it's been great fun learning and feeling more like I'm part of the culture.

The key objective for this new fulfillment center was to start from an empty building and in 60 days put in the equipment and racking, hire quite a few employees, and ramp up the shipments to several thousand packages per day. So, every few days we were interviewing and hiring another four to six new employees, which meant we were constantly doing orientation and training on the operation and their jobs.

The Three Chengs

The first few days after I arrived at the new facility, the manager had hired three ayi, or cleaning ladies, to help us clean up the facility from the construction and get it ready to start operations. Two of them were sisters by the surname of Cheng, and the third one's surname was also Cheng. So we affectionately referred to them as "The Three Chengs."

Every morning when I first arrived and had contact with them, I would say, "Zao sheng hao, ni hao ma?" which simply means "Good morning, how are you?" At first, they would keep their heads down and not even look up at me. They might mumble something softly and inaudibly in reply. But in the Chinese culture, factory workers in general, and women in particular, were not supposed to make eye contact or speak to the "da lao ban," or big boss. And even worse, I was the American da lao ban and the Senior Vice-President of Worldwide Operations.

The Three Chengs had never experienced anything like this before. The big boss or da lao ban was actually smiling at them and speaking to them to say good morning and asking how they were doing.

It took a couple of weeks of consistently doing that every morning, and slowly but surely their heads started to raise up and acknowledge me, then finally responding with the customary "hen hao" (meaning "very well"). And finally, also saying to me, "Ni ne?" which means "And you?"

It may be more understandable and demonstrative in a culture like in China, but I wonder how many of the people that work for you and with you are needing the same kind of acknowledgement and love shown to them as The Three Chengs. From my experience, most of them do. It takes so little, but it means so much.

Over the next couple of months working at the facility every day, I developed quite a strong bond with these ladies and many other employees at the warehouse. The Three Chengs brought me flowers from their garden one morning when they found out I had been sick and was not feeling well. Most of the time none of us could understand what the other one was saying, but we laughed and joked and worked together as people without titles. I think this is the way that God intended it to be. I only wish I had learned this lesson much earlier in my career and practiced it relentlessly.

How many of the people that work for you and with you are needing the same kind of acknowledgement and love shown to them?

One of the things I asked a lady on the administrative staff to do for me was to take a picture of each new employee and then label each picture at the bottom with the name of that employee written in English letters. During the one-hour van ride in the early morning and late in the evening (we worked extremely long hours for those months) from my service apartment to the warehouse facility, I would sit in the back of the van with my laptop and study the faces and memorize the names. Then every day I would be out on the warehouse floor, greeting each employee by name and asking how they were doing. The impact was incredible!

When I finally had to return to the U.S. two weeks before Christmas, they gave me quite a sendoff. First, everyone gathered for a large group picture. Then there were handshakes and hugs with almost everyone. And finally, all 70-plus of them stood outside the building in the rain to wave goodbye. I'm sure you can understand the drops of water leaking out of my eyes as the van drove away. The sense of joy for the opportunity to have this experience and the sense of sadness for having to leave were indescribable.

Don't Give Up

The story that is most pertinent to the subject of this chapter involves a very sharp, well-educated, well-spoken young man by the name of Jian. He had spent two years in the U.K. studying law and spoke American English fluently. He worked for me in handling a lot of important administrative tasks, such as dealing with various government departments and officials, the landlord for the warehouse, assisting with the installation of the IT system, and many other things.

When I left the United States for this adventure, I had prayed that God would bring me people to share my faith with — and He definitely answered that prayer. Early on, Jian had made it clear to us that he was a card-carrying member of the Communist Party in China and therefore was an atheist. I was willing to share with anyone, but once Nan found out about Jian's membership, she emphatically told me to not say a word to him about Jesus. I suspect Nan feared that somehow I would get in big trouble and maybe find myself in jail in a foreign land. I respected her warning with Jian, but my general attitude was that if God wanted me to be arrested and incarcerated in China, then that's what was going to happen. And if God did not want me to be arrested and put in jail, then nothing was going to happen to me. I did use some common sense, but otherwise I tried to shine the light of Christ everywhere I went.

I had taken a few Bibles and other Christian books for my stay in Shanghai, so on the day I was leaving, I apparently gave Jian a copy of a *Daily Walk Bible*. Shortly after my stay in Shanghai, I started my own product sourcing company called Summit Group International and worked a lot with Chinese factories to source the products for my clients. I stayed in touch with Jian mostly by email. Whenever I happened to be in Shanghai, I would arrange to meet him for lunch, dinner, or coffee. We would catch up, and he would tell me about some of the other employees that we worked with at the warehouse. He also did some business for us in China in contacting certain factories when we had a special project. He also carried out legal work on various contracts for me and took care of setting up a Wholly Foreign Owned Entity (WFOE) for a new business in China.

We developed quite a friendship and had great respect for each other. I prayed for him regularly that he would come to know Jesus. Occasionally I would forward an email from a friend with some interesting reading about God or a short video with a subtle but clear message.

Twelve years after I first met Jian in Shanghai, he replied to one of my emails with a short Christian video. He asked me if I remembered the Bible that I had left him when I returned to the U.S. all that time ago. I actually did not remember that very clearly. (I must have done that if he is telling me that I did!) He said that he enjoyed the video and then told me that he had started reading that Bible a few months ago. Are you messing with me? I knew he had moved several times in the Shanghai area over the years, and yet he still had kept that Bible. Frankly, I would not have been surprised if he had thrown it in the trash as soon as my van was out of sight.

I prayed for him regularly that he would come to know Jesus.

Sharing the Gospel on Skype

We arranged a Skype call a few days later, and he told me more of the story. He had started reading in the beginning with Genesis Chapter 1 but (unsurprisingly) had gotten bogged down in Deuteronomy. So he skipped over to reading the New Testament and was now in the Book of John. I was thrilled out of my mind for what God was doing!

Before we ended the call, I told him that I was a member of a Christian businessman's organization and that I had some study materials online that might be helpful to him in understanding what he was reading in the Bible. I was referring to the one-on-one discipleship program that CBMC has developed called "Operation Timothy." It's primarily designed for a new believer but can be used with someone who is seeking. I suggested to him that I would be happy to help him go through the materials. So, every two weeks on Saturday evening Denver time (Sunday morning Shanghai time), we would spend about 60 to 90 minutes on a Skype call talking through Operation Timothy.

The first section of this program asks the question "What is the meaning or purpose of life?" We had a couple of good discussions, and he seemed to be a fast learner. On the third call on December 5, he asked me to share my story about how I became a Christian. So I shared a short version of my testimony and how I had made the decision to accept Jesus Christ as my Lord and Savior. He was very interested and asked some great questions.

Then he said to me what all of us Ambassadors for Christ long to hear: "What do I need to do to have Jesus in my life?" I explained this incredible free gift and what he needed to believe. He said "great," and I prayed him through the sinner's prayer.

I was amazed and ecstatic about the decision he had reached and how God had orchestrated all the details. I told him, "I am so happy for you and your family. You have made the most important decision of your life, and it will never be the same again. You may find this hard to believe, but I have been praying for you almost every day for the last 12 years."

He was completely shocked. "That's incredible," he said. "That must be the Spirit, and that really means a lot to me."

Remember that God is the One who saves, not me. I am His Ambassador, witness, and messenger.

Ask God and Be Intentional

One of the key points about this story is the need to be intentional in keeping in touch with people you know and care about, and also the people that God has brought across your path that He wants you to love and share the Gospel with. All you have to do is ask God how He wants you to do it. It could be a simple text or email message, a phone call, a get-together for coffee, an invite to your house for a BBQ, or a personal visit to catch up. And each time you do one of these things, don't feel under pressure to share the entire Gospel message and lead this person to accept Christ. All we are doing is building the relationship a little at a time, witnessing through our own behavior ("use words only if necessary"), looking for opportunities that God creates to explain more about the ***Good (Great) News***, and loving them as God commanded.

Remember that God is the One who saves, not me. I am His Ambassador, witness, and messenger. And it's all in God's timing. I prayed for 12 years for Jian. I've heard stories of faithful men that kept praying for decades for someone to become a believer. Some of them did and some of them didn't. Your role is to Go, Love, and Share. The rest is up to God, so relax and enjoy the journey and the relationships, ***As You Go***.

Living It Out, *As You Go*

Key Points to Remember

- Pray first that God will bring people to you that you can share your faith with.
- Build relationships a little at a time and love them as God commanded.
- Stay in touch and continue to pray. Be genuinely interested in the other person and what's happening in their life.

What Will I Do?

43. How can I be more intentional about keeping in touch with people I know and care about?

    ____

    ____

    ____

44. Are there times when I try to control the timing instead of trusting God's timing?

    ____

    ____

    ____

45. How can I be more relaxed about sharing my faith and building new relationships?

    ____

    ____

    ____

Summary

Let's Review the Key Steps

1. **Always Start with Prayer** – Ask God to make divine appointments for you every day.
2. **Use Words Only If Necessary** – Let your behavior represent Christ; people are watching.
3. **Let God Transform You** – Become more Christlike in what you think, say, and do.
4. **Be Alert and Available at All Times** – Have your radar on to see those God wants to connect with you.
5. **As You Go, Make Disciples** – Live your life enthusiastically and be willing to engage.
6. **Relationships Matter** – Connect and engage with people, showing care and trust.
7. **Gentleness and Respect** – Relax and have fun shining the Light of Christ.
8. **Stories Are Interesting, Yours and Mine** – Ask open-ended questions and listen to others' stories.
9. **Invitations May Be All You Need** – Meet, greet, and arrange to have coffee.
10. **Stay in Touch and Keep Praying!** – Never give up; hang in there for as long as it takes.

PART 3

Changing Lives, One at a Time!

Can you help one person?

"The least of you will become a thousand, the smallest a mighty nation. I am the LORD; in its time I will do this swiftly."

Isaiah 60:22

"I tell you that in the same way there will be more rejoicing in heaven over one sinner who repents than over ninety-nine righteous persons who do not need to repent."

Luke 15:7

"Make a difference in someone's life every day. It does make a difference. Everyone has the ability to make a difference."

Angie Karan
Australian Blogger

One of the reasons I came to develop this concept of ***As You Go*** and write this book is because God showed me about 15 years ago that I was missing out in a big way on His plan for me to engage with people and share the Gospel. A few years after I started traveling to China, I started having recurring thoughts and dreams of entering the Pearly Gates to meet Jesus and having Him review the highlights of my life. He essentially said, "You know all those wonderful things you are doing in China to share the Gospel and save the souls of a billion people over there? Well, I appreciated your efforts, but I had that one taken care of." Then He continued, "I kept bringing people across your path every day that I wanted you to connect with, and you keep ignoring them because you were too busy trying to save the world. How about just one person at a time? A person that I made a divine appointment for with you."

Yes, Lord. Thanks for showing that to me before I get to Heaven, so I can change my focus and be obedient to Your plan.

There is a poem by Kris Wilder called "*My Friend*" that is a powerful reminder of what Jesus said in Matthew 7:21-23: "Not everyone who says to Me, 'Lord, Lord,' shall enter the kingdom of heaven, but he who does the will of My Father in heaven. Many will say to Me in that day, 'Lord, Lord, have we not prophesied in Your name, cast out demons in Your name, and done many wonders in Your name?' And then I will declare to them, 'I never knew you; depart from Me, you who practice lawlessness!'"

My Friend

My friend, I stand in the judgment now,
And feel that you're to blame somehow.
On earth I walked with you day by day,
And never did you point the way.
You knew the Lord in truth and glory,
But never did you tell the story.
My knowledge then was very dim,
You could have led me safely to Him.
Though we lived together on earth,
You never told me of the second birth.
And now I stand this day condemned,
Because you failed to mention Him.
You taught me many things, that's true.
I called you friend and trusted you.
But I learn now that it's too late.
You could have kept me from this fate.
We walked by day and talked by night,
And yet you showed me not the light.
You let me live and love and die.
You knew I'd never live on high.
Yes, I called you friend in life,
And trusted you through joy and strife.
And yet on coming to the end,
I cannot now call you my friend.

I am committed to avoiding having a friend of mine send me this poem at the end of their life. And I believe all of us would be heartbroken to know that we had plenty of opportunities to share Christ with family and close friends but failed to do so, and when they face Jesus after they die, He says, "Sorry, I don't know you."

Please, please pray for the salvation of your family and close friends, and show them and tell them about Jesus, ***As You Go***.

16

Making Your Life Count!

When I finally realized it's not all about me.

"Let us not become weary in doing good, for at the proper time we will reap a harvest if we do not give up."

Galatians 6:9

"You have blessings. You have gifts. You have passion. You have drive. Get after it; go in there and do something. Try and make every day count."

Kimberly Guilfoyle
American television news personality

For about 20 years, I have traveled to many parts of China for business. After witnessing some of the miraculous growth in Christianity there and because of my great interest in "going and making disciples of all nations," I prayed for God to give me the opportunity to share the Gospel and hopefully lead some of my connections to know Him. And He definitely answered those prayers. I have had some phenomenal experiences in my travels and business dealings, ***As I Go***. Some of those stories are an integral part of this book.

And there have been many, many more experiences and divine appointments during my extensive travels to China and other parts of Asia. I had the feeling that I was somehow making a difference, and I'm certain that it's true for at least a few.

Throwing Starfish Back

But this reminds me of a story that most of you have probably already heard. It's about the young boy on the beach throwing starfish back into the ocean. There are thousands of starfish washed up and stranded on the beach after the tide receded, and they are left there surely to die before the ocean waters rise again to take them back into their ocean home.

A man walking on the beach that morning sees the young lad and says to him, "What are you doing? There are so many starfish here on the beach that are going to die soon — you can't possibly make a difference." The wise, young boy picked up another starfish, turned to the man while holding out his hand to show him the starfish before he tossed it back into the ocean, and said, "It makes a big difference to this one." And so it did.

Who are those starfish in your life? Maybe a family member or a neighbor or a coworker? Or maybe just a new acquaintance that God has brought across your path?

"It makes a big difference to this one." And so it did.

Like almost all of us, I want my life to make a difference, to count for something. So I became passionate about the Great Commission and sharing my faith with anyone who would listen, ***As I Go.***

Check on Your Family and Friends

As I explained at the beginning of Part 3, God showed me clearly that He wanted me to pay attention to the people He was bringing across my path, especially my close family and friends. And He told me that I had been too busy trying to save a billion people in China and had essentially ignored many of them.

Wow! Have you ever worked on a grand scheme for something, only to realize that the thing you were supposed to do was right under your nose? Well, that was definitely the case for me. Did I immediately stop doing anything in China or other parts of the world when the opportunity presented itself? Of course not! I continued with as much excitement and passion as ever before.

But what I did do was take an inventory of the people closest to me. And I started having my radar on when I was at or near home. I went down the list of friends and family members in my life and tried to assess where they stood regarding their salvation. And then I went about intentionally praying for them and looking for the right opportunity to ask them some very important questions.

Bill was one of those people on my list. He and I had gone to high school together in Milledgeville, Georgia, and he had introduced me to Nan during my senior year. (By the way, thankfully, Nan has forgiven him for that.) Bill was one of the nicest, most generous people I ever knew and was a well-respected citizen of my hometown. His wife, Patsy, was a strong believer and a regular churchgoer, while Bill seldom went with her. So, I had my doubts about where he stood with Jesus and whether he would be with us in heaven.

And then I went about intentionally praying for them and looking for the right opportunity to ask them some very important questions.

During one of his visits to Colorado to spend some time with Nan and me, I had the opportunity to ask Bill that all-important question about his belief in Christ one afternoon while our wives were out shopping. With gentleness and respect for our friendship, I shared where I believed I would be going when I died and told him that I cared so much about him and wanted him to be there, too. Praise God, he gave me the right answer!

And I'm so grateful that I could rest in peace about where he would be, because he died a few years later at age

57 from the third type of cancer he had battled. I sometimes think about how awful it would have been if I had spent all this time over the years with my dear friend and he had not shared what he believed, so that when he died I would not have known if he would be in heaven when I get there. And worse than anything would it have been for me not to know, and then when I get to heaven not to find him there.

Like almost all of us, I want my life to make a difference, to count for something.

I asked several other people in my life including my favorite uncle who was like a second dad to me. He gave me the right answer. But my aunt in California did not, and a couple of other friends did not. So, I am praying for them and seeking to reach them before it's too late.

I also asked a dear friend who lived in the apartment above us with his wife when Nan and I first got married. That has been a lifelong friendship. David told me that he grew up in the church but had been turned off by how judgmental the attitude had been. So he had drifted away and was not quite sure what he believed anymore. After a weekend visit with him at their home in Atlanta, I sent him a devotional book and a nice note, explaining that I really wanted him to be in heaven with us one day. It seemed to have an impact, and he has been reading the devotional and praying for several years now.

Jim Petersen of the Navigators says, "We step over people we have related to for years and go to people we've never laid eyes on before."

So many Christians think that sharing their faith means talking to strangers about Jesus. And it does. But what about the people closest to you? The people you love the most — parents, children, aunts and uncles, cousins, dear friends. Selfishly, aren't these the people you definitely want to have in heaven with you for eternity? If each of us would just focus on showing the love of Christ and engaging for the cause of the Gospel with this group of people, think how much bigger the Kingdom would be.

Jim Petersen of the Navigators says, "We step over people we have related to for years and go to people we've never laid eyes on before."

Can You Impact One Person?

In fact, if every person who confesses to be a follower of Christ would impact one person with the ***Good (Great) News*** and God changed their hearts to believe in Christ, that would be a ginormous number of people. Organizations that track this kind of information tell us that there are about 2 billion Christians in the world. My experience is that quite a few of those people might believe in God but do not truly have a saving faith in Christ.

So, what if it's half that number, 1 billion people? And each of them loved on one person to lead them to accept Christ? That's 1 billion new believers! And what if those new believers shared with another person? Wow!

One person — just one person you know and love! Can you do that? Of course, you can. I'm not asking anyone to become the next Billy Graham and evangelize millions of people around the world. I'm asking that you engage intentionally, proactively, with love and gentleness and respect in your heart, to share the ***Greatest News Ever*** in the history of the world with someone close to you.

Make your life count, even if it's with only one person, ***As You Go***.

Living It Out, *As You Go*

Key Points to Remember

- Don't forget about the salvation of your family and close friends.
- Making your life count for something might be a lot easier than you think.
- If every believer would love on just one person to lead them to accept Christ, a billion people could join the Kingdom.

What Will I Do?

46. Who are the starfish in my life? How can I make a difference?

____

____

____

47. Who are my family members and close friends that have not accepted Christ as their Lord and Savior?

____

____

____

48. How can I broach the subject to find out where my family and friends stand with Jesus?

____

____

____

17

Reaching the Unconvinced!

Evangelism — Shining the Light

"While I am in the world, I am the light of the world."

John 9:5

"Every Christian is either a missionary or an impostor."

Charles Spurgeon
English Baptist Preacher, "Prince of the Preachers"

"If you had the cure for cancer, wouldn't you share it? You have the cure for death... Get out there and share it!"

Kirk Cameron
TV and Movie Actor, Christian Evangelist

Changes in Culture Since the 50s

Let's face it: The term "evangelism" or "evangelical" is not a very popular or politically correct label in our culture today. Surveys show that an evangelical person has a lower approval rating than Congress, and that's pretty low. For many people, it conjures up images of the "hellfire and damnation" preacher on the cable channel and memories of Christians who didn't talk or act much like Christians.

These unchristian images that are prevalent all around us form the picture that most Americans have of what the Christian faith is all about. And understandably, they want nothing to do with it. In fact, they don't even want to talk to you about the subject because of these bad images seared in their minds.

It wasn't but a few decades ago, in the post-World War II generation, that Christianity was viewed much more positively in our society. Families went to church, most of us learned about the major stories in the Bible, and Christian values and beliefs were well respected by most. It was much easier to talk about faith during the decades of the 50s through the 70s.

Surveys show that an evangelical person has a lower approval rating than Congress, and that's pretty low.

And then things started to change — partly because the Church was not leading, but mostly because our culture was experiencing dramatic changes in views about gender identity, sexual orientation, marriage, abortion, and a whole host of other issues.

Because so many people were familiar with Christianity back then, you could focus on reaping the harvest by using somewhat of a salesman's approach to sharing the Gospel. And that was great. But times have drastically changed, and now the salesman's approach is generally offensive and ineffective. We need to be more focused on sowing and cultivating the Gospel message in our relationships.

Lifestyle Evangelism

To me, this term, evangelism, is simply about sharing the Gospel of Jesus Christ, the ***Good (Great) News***! It's simply doing what Jesus commanded in Matthew 28:19.

A key focus of this book is how to be effective as a marketplace ambassador or evangelist, ***As You Go***. In fact, the 10 chapters in Part 2 — *What Does "As You Go" Look Like?* — have been all about the various steps in becoming a better Ambassador for Christ in the world. A better way to think about this concept is "reaching the unconvinced." In this country, a lot of people have (or think they have) heard all about Christianity and the message of salvation. And maybe they have. But they have just not been convinced yet that it's true and the answer to their soul spending eternity with God, instead of separated from God in that "lake of fire."

I believe that one of the best ways to think about living out the Great Commission is to consider it a lifestyle. Dave Rathkamp, Area Director of CBMC in Houston, describes that *Lifestyle Evangelism* "is just loving people, it's being with people and caring where they are. And caring not just for their soul, but for their humanness and being alongside them to help."

A better way to think about this concept is "reaching the unconvinced."

CBMC has developed a wonderful program on Lifestyle Evangelism called "Living Proof Adventure." It contains 12 principles that will help you develop your skills in being "Living Proof." Each lesson has short videos and great discussion questions from experts on the subject. I would highly recommend that you check it out and maybe use it in your small group or Bible study.

The process of reaching out to another person can be thought of by using the example of farming. The three main steps in farming are cultivating, sowing, and harvesting. The farmer tills the soil and plants the seeds. God does the growing, and then at the right time, the farmer harvests the crop.

The farmer in most cases is involved in the entire process. In doing Lifestyle Evangelism, it's not a requirement to complete the process resulting in someone accepting Christ as their Lord and Savior. It's a real blessing when God allows you to do that, but He may only want you to be involved in one part of this process. He may have other plans for the timing and people He wants to use.

I believe that we should think about this process as "bringing a person one step closer" to giving their life to Christ. By the way, understanding that takes all the pressure off. I no longer have to feel like a failure if I don't close the deal and notch my belt with a new convert. It's in God's hands; He just wants me to participate with Him. But Christ is not asking if you'd like to be involved — He's commanded you to.

A helpful tool in assessing where a person is in their spiritual journey is the chart on the next page called a Spiritual Awareness Assessment, adapted by CBMC from "The Engel Scale" by James Engle. Once you have a sense of where they are and what they currently believe, then you are in a much better position to know how to approach them and what to say when you share the Gospel message with them.

The process of reaching out to another person can be thought of by using the example of farming.

As I mentioned before, for some reason we think that the Great Commission can be outsourced to the pastors and missionaries. Someone else, not me. But just before Christ ascended into heaven, He gave His final instructions to us. He told YOU and all other believers to "go and make disciples."

God's on the Airplane Again

One of my good friends and fellow Ambassadors for Christ is Marty Campfield, who also lives here in Colorado. He shared this story with me about how he is living out the Great Commission, ***As He Goes***.

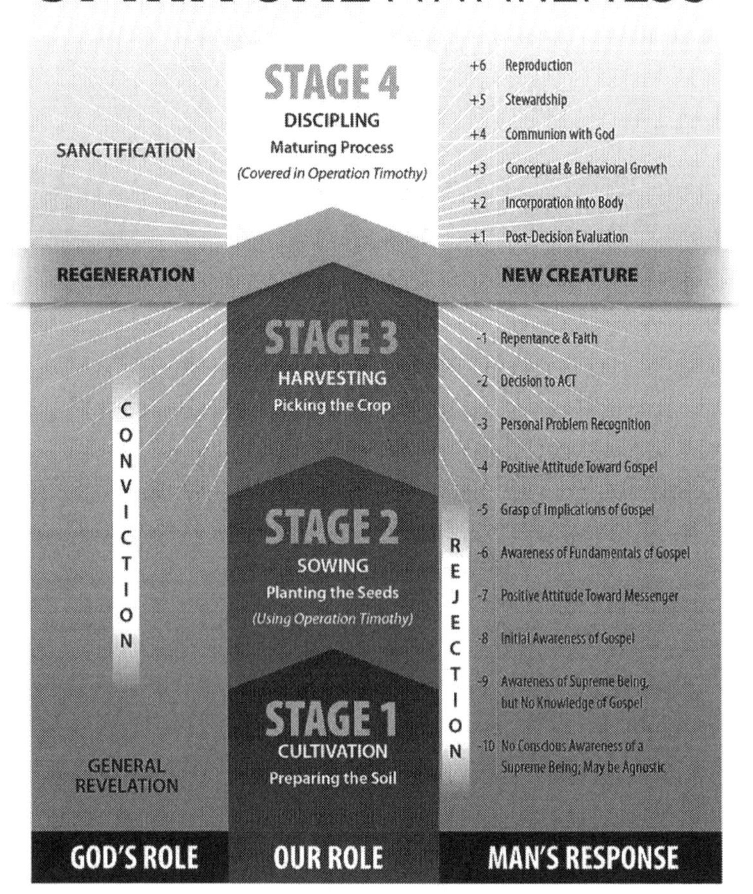
SPIRITUAL AWARENESS
SANCTIFICATION
STAGE 4
DISCIPLING
Maturing Process
(Covered in Operation Timothy)
+6 Reproduction
+5 Stewardship
+4 Communion with God
+3 Conceptual & Behavioral Growth
+2 Incorporation into Body
+1 Post-Decision Evaluation
REGENERATION
NEW CREATURE
STAGE 3
HARVESTING
Picking the Crop
-1 Repentance & Faith
-2 Decision to ACT
-3 Personal Problem Recognition
-4 Positive Attitude Toward Gospel
-5 Grasp of Implications of Gospel
-6 Awareness of Fundamentals of Gospel
-7 Positive Attitude Toward Messenger
-8 Initial Awareness of Gospel
-9 Awareness of Supreme Being, but No Knowledge of Gospel
-10 No Conscious Awareness of a Supreme Being; May be Agnostic
CONVICTION
STAGE 2
SOWING
Planting the Seeds
(Using Operation Timothy)
REJECTION
STAGE 1
CULTIVATION
Preparing the Soil
GENERAL REVELATION
GOD'S ROLE
OUR ROLE
MAN'S RESPONSE

Here's Marty's story:

"I took my seat in the back of the plane against the window and was soon joined by a young husband and wife from Atlanta. I introduced myself, and immediately the young lady (who it turned out worked in HR and spent her days interviewing people) seated beside me began questioning me rapid-fire: 'Who are you? What do you do? Where do you work? Are you flying home tonight? Where do you live?' After a short time, we had discussed the answers to most of these questions.

In one of my answers I mentioned God, and immediately she said, 'Wow, there you go testifying in the middle of your answer.' Her reaction took me by surprise, so I said, 'Well, that's an interesting response. What prompted that?' She said, 'Oh well, you're talking about God, and I'm a person of faith, so I find that interesting.' She shared that she and her husband were Christians from a large church in Atlanta and were flying up to Baltimore to go to a friend's wedding. We had a little more small talk, and then I closed my eyes and drifted off to sleep.

When I awoke, I noticed she was reading a book called Evangelism Explosion. *I said, 'I see you're reading a book about evangelism — that is my heart's passion in life.' She was interested to hear more, and so I was able to share with her a few stories of my experiences with God working to bring the* ***Good News*** *to people as I step out in faith, open my mouth to share, and the Holy Spirit does the rest.*

She and her husband had been studying this book and

were learning how to do evangelism in their church in Atlanta. So I shared with her many of my concepts and experiences of getting to the point within less than a minute and seeing the Holy Spirit move in mighty ways. I explained the importance of quoting God's Word and getting it in front of people either by my business card or a tract or verbally.

I also told her that I found the most powerful thing is to get God's Word out there because it never returns void, and the Holy Spirit can use it so powerfully to convict and reach people instantly on the spot. She really liked that approach and was taking notes as we talked.

After an hour of great conversation, our flight began to approach Baltimore. I have found many times on these flights that once you're coming in to land, great things begin to happen. I'm not sure why this is.

As we landed and pulled up to the gate, the lady in the row of seats in front of us stood up and turned around to face us, kneeling on her seat and leaning on her elbows on the top of the backrest. I looked at her and was a bit concerned because she was staring right at me, and I was still seated below her. I had no idea what she was about to say. There were about 20 people within easy earshot of what she was about to say. She then said loudly, 'I need to say something to the two of you because I could not avoid hearing your conversation during this flight.

'Normally, I'm listening to music on every flight, but this morning my phone screen broke. I was unable to navigate to my music, so I was here without ear

phones. I tried to sleep, but I could not avoid hearing everything that you two were saying. The things that you're talking about with God and evangelism have impacted me greatly. I have not been walking with God the way I should be lately. I needed to hear all this, and it's obvious to me now that there was a reason that my phone broke this morning. I have been so moved by what you two have talked about and how you have put God first in your lives, that sitting here in the seat tonight on this flight I have decided to rededicate my life to Christ! Thank you both for what you have shared tonight — it has meant so much to me.'

I then looked her square in the eyes and said out loud, 'Do you have the Lord Jesus Christ as your personal Lord and Savior?' She said, 'Yes, I do!' and we exchanged a high-five.

People all around us were listening, and this was the most awesome thing I have seen yet on an airplane. As soon as I stood up from my seat, I looked down, and the lady in front of me was calling somebody, recounting to them what had just happened, and telling them that she had made a new commitment to God. The couple beside me was obviously moved as these were the firstfruits of their beginning adventures in evangelism. They told me they were going back to Atlanta on Sunday and would be sharing our conversation and this experience with the people in their small group at church.

I can only imagine how many people this story will reach and the impact and ripple effects of this experience when God was at work. It's totally to the glory of God how He

> *orchestrated the four of us to be in those exact seats on the plane. I also think of all the people around us, who may have also been powerfully impacted in a positive way. How many of them will share this encounter — how many people will be touched when it's all said and done?"*

Marty's story is another great example of how God will use you to impact peoples' lives if you will step out in faith, open your mouth, and let God take it from there after He has already orchestrated the circumstances leading to this divine appointment, ***As You Go***.

Living It Out, *As You Go*

Key Points to Remember

- Christianity was viewed much more positively in our society for several decades after World War II.
- A better way to think about this concept is "reaching the unconvinced."
- The Spiritual Awareness Chart is useful in determining where someone is on their spiritual journey.
- Let God use you to impact peoples' lives by stepping out in faith, opening your mouth, and letting God take it from there.

What Will I Do?

49. Where am I on the Spiritual Awareness Chart?

____

____

____

50. How would I assess my spouse and close family and friends? How will that assessment influence reaching them?

____

____

____

51. The next time I'm on a flight, can I start a conversation like Marty did with the person sitting next to me?

____

____

____

18

Discipling All Nations

"Teaching them to obey everything I have commanded you."

"Then he said to his disciples, 'The harvest is plentiful, but the workers are few. Ask the Lord of the harvest, therefore, to send out workers into his harvest field.'"

Matthew 9:37-38

"Christianity without discipleship is Christianity without Christ."

Dietrich Bonhoeffer
German pastor and theologian,
author of **The Cost of Discipleship**

"To get nations back on their feet, we must first get down on our knees."

Billy Graham
Evangelist to the World

All the discussion in this book so far has been about sharing your faith, being an Ambassador, reaching the unconvinced, engaging with people, loving them well, being the best example of Christ, etc. And for sure, it has been a deliberate effort in the previous chapters to encourage, empower, and compel you to "get in the game" and to start the process of living out the Great Commission — "to spark a conversation that impacts eternity"!

Most Christians believe that the operative word in Jesus' command in Matthew 28:19 is "Go." I have tried to make the case that His intended meaning of "Go" is to follow His command "***As You Go***" along your way, every day and everywhere.

It turns out that the Great Commission is more about discipleship than evangelism.

"Go and Make"

But now I need to make an important clarification: The word "Go" in the Greek is not the right tense to be the operative word in this passage. The word "make" is the correct tense to be the action word in this command. Jesus is talking about "making disciples of all nations." Actually, it turns out that the Great Commission is more about discipleship than evangelism.

The problem is that it's hard to tell where one leaves off and the other one begins. Jim Petersen of the Navigators, in a video from the CBMC Living Proof Adventure series, comments, "I don't make a big distinction between evangelism and discipleship. Because of the dynamics of both activities, I think the line between the two is really blurred and should be that way."

My main point from the beginning is that 97% of believers are not doing the "Go" part of the Great Commission by getting off their "Buts" and engaging with people by showing them and telling them about Jesus. You must do the "***As You Go***" part before you can do the "make disciples" part, even though the lines are blurred. You can teach someone different behaviors and attitudes that are more Christ-like before they become a believer, but it's after they believe that the real heart transformation starts to take place.

Newspaper columnist Cal Thomas, who is a Christian, challenged the Church to look at the quality of its discipleship. He wrote that the problem in the culture is not the abortionists. It isn't the pornographers or drug dealers or criminals. It's the undisciplined, un-discipled, disobedient, and biblically ignorant Christians.

"I don't make a big distinction between evangelism and discipleship."

Wow, that's a strong statement, but I think he's right. And sadly, I'm one of those Christians that need to be more obedient and biblically mature.

I think many believers are unclear about what's involved in discipleship. So let me provide a definition that might help.

What Is Discipleship?

I really like this definition from an organization called All About Following Jesus: "Discipleship is teaching biblical precepts, while modeling and guiding others toward living righteously as followers of Jesus Christ. This should be a cyclical process — meaning once we are discipled, we are to disciple others, and so on. One of the most important characteristics of being a disciple (a student or pupil) is to develop an intimate relationship with God through Christ rather than just learning about Him. Discipleship equips the Christian with God's Word, prayer, doctrine, worship, encouragement, and service."

How Are We Doing?

Christianity is the fastest growing religious group in the world, with 25 million new converts annually. But that's not what's happening in America. I think part of the problem is that we have mistranslated the Great Commission. When Jesus told His followers 2,000 years ago to "go into all the world and make disciples," we thought He said, "Go into all the world and build churches."

In America we can build churches. We can afford to and we like to. We can build big, beautiful buildings, and they make us feel successful. But that's not what Jesus told us to do.

He said, "Go and make disciples," and He would build His Church. In Matthew 16:18, Jesus said, "I will build my church, and all the powers of hell will not conquer it."

If I asked a hundred pastors in America "What was Jesus' last command to His disciples?" few, if any of them, would not be able to answer. If fact, most could quote His command word for word. But if then I asked them to name their disciples, I might get blank stares. Even the pastors and church leaders, for the most part, are not obedient to one of the Great Commands that Jesus gave us.

This is the Great Omission in the Great Commission: making disciples!

Jesus said, "I will build my church, and all the powers of hell will not conquer it".

How Did Jesus Do It?

Throughout the New Testament, Jesus shows us all about living a Christlike life by teaching, preaching, sharing, and modeling how to be like Him. So, let's think about what He did to make disciples:

- First, He called them. He took His disciples out of their former lifestyle into a new lifestyle — a lifestyle of discipleship.
- He spent lots of time with them, walking and sleeping and eating and doing life together.
- He taught them how to pray.
- He asked great questions and challenged the conventional wisdom of the day.
- He responded differently than expected in many situations.
- He taught them through stories and parables.

- He modeled appropriate behaviors for a Christ follower, like washing their feet.
- He occasionally spoke to big crowds, but He spent most of His time investing in the lives of a few.
- He spent three and a half years discipling a few men and then sent them out to do the same and disciple others.
- He showed them His values, priorities, emotions, attitude, and commitment.

Jesus didn't completely ignore the big crowds; He spoke to them and showed them compassion. But His approach to reaching the masses was obviously to build into the lives of a few and trust the miracle of multiplication that occurs when we use the biblical method.

So, Matthew 28:18-20, referred to as the Great Commission, is the one of the final instructions or commands Jesus gave His disciples before His ascension into heaven. It summarizes His purpose for coming to earth and His purpose for the Church for centuries to come. It concisely states His complete intention for every sincere Christ follower. Of all the things happening in heaven and on earth today, this command is one of the most important.

Discipleship is not an option — it's a command of Christ! It was one of His final commands: to make disciples. And the discipleship process is not complete until the disciples we make are making other disciples. It's the wonderful process of building His Church or Kingdom. It's not more Bible studies and Christian conferences; it's making disciples of all nations, ***As You Go***.

Living It Out, *As You Go*

Key Points to Remember

- It turns out that the Great Commission is more about discipleship than evangelism.
- You must do the "As You Go" part before you can do the "make disciples" part.
- Review the list in this chapter of how Jesus made disciples.
- Discipleship is not an option — it's a command of Christ!

What Will I Do?

52. Who immediately comes to mind when I think about someone I know who needs to be discipled?

    ____

    ____

    ____

53. Do I agree that every believer should be discipled and should be discipling another person?

    ____

    ____

    ____

54. Am I willing to enter into a close personal discipleship relationship for several years?

    ____

    ____

    ____

19

Operation Timothy

Discipleship and Spiritual Reproduction

"And the things you have heard me say in the presence of many witnesses entrust to reliable people who will also be qualified to teach others."

2 *Timothy* 2:2

"By God's design, he has wired his children for spiritual reproduction. He has woven into the fabric of every single Christian's DNA a desire and ability to reproduce."

David Platte

Pastor of McLean Bible Church, NYT Bestselling Author

A group of Christian businessmen had started meeting at the home of a very successful businessman in Denver, and after about a year, the group had grown to between 40 and 45 men who'd meet from 6:30 to 8 a.m. every Friday morning in the finished basement of this man's house in a wealthy suburb of Denver.

Jim Sigler, my dear friend and co-laborer in Christ, and I had been invited to this businessman's home to share our knowledge of evangelism and discipleship with this group for three Fridays. Jim and I took turns sharing various aspects of the key elements in being more effective marketplace ambassadors and in discipling men. During one of the sessions that Jim was teaching, I sat in the audience near the back of the room on a folding chair.

The focus is one-on-one, life-on-life discipleship between a more mature believer, called a Paul, and a less mature believer, called a Timothy.

A young man in his early to mid-30s was sitting on my left. His name was Brett. We were asked by Jim to pair off and do a simple exercise as part of the program. So I turned to my left and paired off with Brett. We spent the next 15 minutes getting to know each other a little bit and doing the exercise. It seemed to me that we hit it off rather nicely, and something he mentioned about his dad reminded me of my dad and how his life had ended.

On the drive back home that morning, I began to think about my encounter with Brett, and I believe that the Holy

Spirit suggested to me that Brett might be a good candidate to engage in the CBMC "Operation Timothy" discipleship program.

Operation Timothy is a wonderful discipleship tool originally developed by CBMC with the help of the Navigators in the late 70s. Updated and improved four times since then, this material has proven effective thousands and thousands of times to help a person grow in their faith and better become the person God created them to be. The focus is one-on-one, life-on-life discipleship between a more mature believer, called a Paul, and a less mature believer, called a Timothy. It can also be used quite effectively for an unconvinced person who is seeking, as I mentioned earlier about my friend in Shanghai.

So, later on I called Brett at his office and told him how much I enjoyed meeting him earlier that morning and how it seemed that we had some things in common. Then I told him that it occurred to me on the drive home that he might be interested in getting together to study the Operation Timothy materials. He said, "What is Operation Timothy?" I said, "Don't you remember the material that Jim and I discussed at the previous Friday's meeting?" He replied, "No, I'm sorry. I was not able to attend the meeting last week."

"Oh, so I'm asking you to do something you've never heard about. Well, how about if we meet for coffee next week and I'll explain it to you?" So we did.

Brett and I started meeting almost every week at an Einstein Bros. Bagels near his office at 6 a.m. for about an hour to an hour and a half. We were able to get to know each other much better, and we became quite good friends over time. Brett had recently started a new job with a wealth management firm in the position where only 10% of the new hires make it through the first year. So he was under a lot of pressure, and he was working really hard because he truly was serious about making it as an investment broker.

Because he was just starting in this job, the firm was providing a monthly draw, but it was not that much. So, money was tight for Brett and his wife and two young girls, adding even more pressure to his situation.

The love for his family was very evident, and he was overwhelmed at the thought of letting them down.

For many weeks he would tell me how he felt like he was in the middle of a war and hunkered down in his bunker with bullets flying all around him. He didn't know if this career change had been a good idea, and he was constantly concerned that his decision was going to be a huge setback for him and his family. The love for his family was very evident, and he was overwhelmed at the thought of letting them down.

We began with Book 1 of Operation Timothy and discussed first the purpose and meaning of life. "Why are you here? What is your purpose? How do you define success?" Powerful questions that all of us have to deal with at some point in our lives. We continued on through the chapters in Book 1 to talk about "Is the Bible credible?" and "Who is Jesus Christ?" and many other topics about life and Christian faith.

Brett seemed eager to learn more about his newfound faith. I learned that it had only been a few weeks before we met that he surrendered his life to Christ as his Lord and Savior on a men's ski trip in the Colorado mountains. He was a baby Christian and needed to be nourished and encouraged and loved and supported as he grew in his faith and trust in Jesus.

"Why are you here? What is your purpose? How do you define success?"

He needed to be taught and discipled by a man who was at least a little further down the road on his spiritual path than Brett. Someone who would come alongside and "do life" with another man. Not just teach him some Christian principles from the Bible, but model it for him as much as possible. And to show him that you are willing to get into the messes of life and that you care enough to have his back and are available at any hour of the day or night to help him.

Just a reminder again of this adage: "People don't care how much you know until they know how much you care." It's so true! And when you show someone that you don't have another agenda in meeting with them, and when they see that you truly will provide a safe place to talk about anything going on in their lives, then many times you will be developing a friendship for a lifetime.

One of the key reasons why I love to disciple other men is that I missed that step for a long time after giving my life to Christ. As I mentioned earlier, when I was 17 years old and a freshman at Georgia Tech, I went to about three meetings of Campus Crusade for Christ. I don't remember anything about how I got there or who I met. But I do very clearly remember praying the sinner's prayer to accept Jesus as my Savior like it happened yesterday.

A short time later I was baptized at the church in my hometown that my high school sweetheart, Nan, and her family attended.

"People don't care how much you know until they know how much you care."

But nobody came along to disciple or mentor this young, baby believer. I don't know if I forgot about the guys at Campus Crusade or they forgot about me. I was putting myself through school, so I was working 30 to 40 hours per week at the student center, mopping floors and taking 16 to 18 credit hours per quarter. I didn't have time to pursue growing in my faith, and plus, I didn't have a clue about the process. I guessed maybe it would be by osmosis or going to church.

I graduated from Georgia Tech in three and a half years and got married to Nan at the beginning of my senior year. I took a job with a textile manufacturer in Georgia for my first year and then went to work for a consulting firm in Atlanta for the next six. There I became the youngest associate/partner in the history of the company at age 26. And generally, things were going really well. I moved to two other companies as a Vice President, quickly moving up the corporate ladder and doing better than frankly I could have imagined.

I wandered in the wilderness, chasing success in business for 23 years before God woke me up and brought me to my knees. First, my dad died suddenly at age 63, and my life went into a tailspin. I would get up early in the morning before work and walk in the neighborhood, crying my eyes out, pleading with God to tell me why this had happened and why my life was such a mess.

A few months later, I lost my big, corporate job and was given a pittance of severance pay. We had too much debt, small savings, and a big lifestyle. Somehow, we lived for nine months on nine weeks of severance pay. God took care of us, and I had an amazing peace during most of this time.

The main point here is that I went without being discipled for 23 years and had not developed a close relationship with Christ. I can only imagine how my life would have been better and more productive if a Christian man had come alongside me during those years. Of course, God had a plan and His timing is perfect, so I don't have any regrets. I wouldn't have this story to tell if my life had been different during those 23 years. But it gave me a desire that turned into a passion for "reaching a man right where he is and helping him become the man God created him to be."

Love, Purpose, and Trust

Let's get back to the rest of the story about Brett: As we kept meeting for months, which turned into a few years, he was definitely growing in his understanding of the Christian life and in his faith in God. But he was still going through very stressful times with work and other aspects of his life. He was in the small percentage that made it through the first year as a new broker, but now he was fighting to keep his job and make enough money to keep the bill collectors away from his doorstep. He told me that less than 10% of the people starting out in his field are still there after 3 years.

I remember on a number of occasions reminding him of essentially this: God loves you more than you can imagine, and God has a plan and purpose for your life, and God wants you to trust Him with everything, and God wants you to let Him take care of you. As Brett was fighting the battles of work and life, we constantly kept coming back to these truths.

God loves you more than you can imagine, and God has a plan and purpose for your life.

We kept going with our regular meetings for several years and then moved to getting together about once a month. His hard work and growing trust in God began to pay off, and he got over the hump. He was making decent money, and his future looked bright.

Several years later we had lunch again, and somehow our discussion turned to those early days when we started meeting and how he was "in the trenches" fighting for his life. Then Brett shared something with me that totally stunned me: "During those difficult years at work, I was getting so stressed and so hopeless that things would ever get better that I started to plan a way to 'take one for the team.'" Of course, what he meant was committing suicide, but making it look like it wasn't suicide, so his wife and girls would be OK financially from the insurance.

He was not thinking about the tremendous harm he would do to his family by having his girls grow up without a dad and overcoming the feeling that they were partly the cause of him doing this. And so many other terrible consequences. But he just didn't know another way out of the pain.

Then he made a mind-blowing statement to me. He said, "If you and I had not been meeting every week, and if you had not kept telling me that God loves me and has a plan for my life and how I just need to trust Him, I would have killed myself for sure several years ago. You saved my life!"

Wow!!! What did he just say? I had no idea. My heart was overflowing with gratitude and amazement for what God had done through sharing my life with another man for one hour a week.

Well, this story does not end here. There's another wonderful part to it.

Teacher Becomes Student

A few years later I was going through a very difficult time in my life. We had somehow managed to survive the global recession of 2008 to 2012. Some of my friends told me that their business was off by 30%. I told them no, my business WAS 30%. (Guess what? That's not even close to a break-even point.) We almost lost our business during those years. A lot of other business and personal situations were also going on, and I was getting extremely tired, frustrated, hopeless, and literally depressed.

But it gave me a desire that turned into a passion for "reaching a man right where he is and helping him become the man God created him to be."

Finally, one Thursday night Nan and I had the worse fight I can ever remember. And I quickly spiraled into a major funk. I cried half the night and got almost no sleep. When the alarm went off at 5:30 a.m., I was in no mood to get out of bed. But I remembered that I had a serious obligation to take care of that morning. I was on the board of a children's charity here in Denver, and we were having the annual golf tournament to raise money for this worthy cause. I had already paid my $200 and had invited someone else to join me. As bad as I felt, I just couldn't skip this event.

I somehow managed to get dressed and leave the house that morning, but I was in such a dark and difficult place, I honestly didn't know if I was coming back home.

On the 30-minute drive to the golf course, my cell phone rang and it was Brett. He seldom calls me; I'm normally the one initiating the calls. So my first thought was that there must be something really wrong. When I answered, he simply said, "Hey man, how are you doing?"

I let out a deep sigh and replied to him, "Not so good. Actually, I'm really in a tough place this morning and I don't know what to do."

Brett said, "You don't sound so good. I was thinking

about you on my drive to the office this morning and felt God prompting me to call you. Can we meet somewhere right away?"

"No, I can't do that", I responded. "I am headed to play in a charity golf event for the organization that I'm a board member of. I won't be finished until about 2 o'clock this afternoon."

Brett forcefully said, "OK, I'll come out your way and meet you at 2:30 at the Starbucks." I told him that I didn't know if I could be there or not. He insisted that there would be no debate: I should be there to meet him at 2:30.

"I was thinking about you on my drive to the office this morning and felt God prompting me to call you."

As I'm looking back on this, the other thing that seemed odd is that I had never met Brett at any other time of the day than early in the morning or at lunchtime. And because of his work demands, I always drove over near his office because my time was more flexible. But today he was going to leave the office in the early afternoon and drive about 25 minutes out near where I would be.

I don't have any idea how I managed to get through 18 holes of golf and lunch and the ceremony to give out the prizes afterwards. I was so tired and numb and down, that it was a miracle I got through it. Now even more exhausted, I drove to meet my dear friend, Brett, for coffee. In some ways, there was a little bit of excitement that he cared so much about me, but there was a lot of uncertainty about what I would be able to share with him.

He was waiting for me at the coffee shop and greeted me with a big hug. Even though I had been transparent with him over the years and had shared many struggles and situations with him, this was definitely different, and I think he knew it. I had always been the mentor, the father figure, the teacher and coach, and he had been my student. Now suddenly our roles were reversed.

He asked me in a very concerned way about what had happened and what was going on. So I shared my story about the recent events and challenges that were about to push me off the cliff. I was hurting so much that it was all I could do to fight back the tears welling up in my eyes, and I had to pause and regroup several times during my explanation.

When I finished sharing with him, he said, "Wow, I just knew something was seriously wrong this morning, and I'm so sorry." Then he continued with confidence and sincerity like never before: "I need to tell you something really important. God loves you more than you can imagine, and God has a plan and purpose for your life. God wants you to trust him with everything, and God wants you to let Him take care of you."

As I listened to these familiar words coming out of his mouth, I knew he was right and that I needed so badly to hear them. I soaked it up and took a deep breath, pausing for a minute to let it truly sink in.

I had always been the mentor, the father figure, the teacher and coach, and he had been my student. Now suddenly our roles were reversed.

Then I said to him, "Who in the world told you that crap?"

"You did!" he quickly replied. We both smiled and nodded in agreement.

While I may not have been in quite the dark place of planning suicide as he had been a few years earlier, I definitely was in a bad place, and my meeting with Brett that afternoon clearly had a big impact on my life. I will be forever grateful that my Timothy, my student, my friend, and my brother in Christ stepped up to lead and follow God's prompting to engage in real life with my serious need that day.

We all need more real, authentic, caring relationships like the one I have with Brett. Our lives and the world would be a better place for it.

So, seek to engage and develop those kinds of real relationships, ***As You Go***.

Spiritual Reproduction

How can I possibly reach so many unconvinced people in the world if I try to do it one person at a time? When we think about how to impact millions and billions of lives for Christ, our first (and often only) thought is to build some big organization or develop some large movement. And there's nothing wrong with speaking to a large crowd at your church, or having a Christian television show with a large following, or sponsoring poor children in countries around the world and sharing the Gospel with them. All of these and many other ministries have a role to play and can have a very positive impact.

But is this the model that Jesus recommended to share the Gospel with the unconvinced everywhere and make disciples of all the nations? No, it's not. The model Jesus used and the one that He wants us to use is to disciple a person, who in turn will disciple another person, and on and on.

So, what would happen if you discipled someone in year one and that person discipled another person in year two?

But won't that process of one person at a time take forever to reach millions and billions? Yes, if you are the only one doing it. But if you use the power of duplication and multiplication, amazing things can happen.

Would you rather have $1 million today, or one penny today doubled every day for the next 30 days? It's very tempting to take the $1 million on day one and live financially free from then on. But you would be making a big mistake by selecting that option.

The one penny per day doubled for 30 days is a much better option. After one week, when your total is 64 cents, you might be thinking that you made a really bad decision. Even after another week (now 14 days), you're getting more concerned because the total is only $81.92. On the 21st day you might be feeling a tiny bit better with a total of

$10,485.76. But you could have taken the $1 million on day one, so you probably start to get that sick feeling in your stomach like you missed a huge opportunity.

The math of multiplication is amazing! Go ahead and do the calculations from day 21 to day 30. Nine days later the $10,485.76 will have increased to $10,737,418.24.

So, what would happen if you discipled someone in year one and that person discipled another person in year two? If you continue that process for ten years, a total of 1,024 people will be discipled. Isaiah 60:22 says, "One shall become a thousand." Sounds to me like the biblical model for multiplication and spiritual reproduction.

Let's take it one step further: What if this same process continued multiplying for the next 10 years? The total number of people discipled would be 1,048,576 — over a million people! You started with 1 person 20 years ago and reach over 1 million.

Now it gets really exciting! If we continue this process for another 10 years, or a third decade, the total number of people discipled will be 1,073,741,824. Over 1 billion people! Are you kidding me?

Do you think the world would be a different place if 30 years from now there were 1 billion new believers who had been discipled? What if that first person discipled two people each year and the process was duplicated? The numbers would double to over 2 billion people.

So, why hasn't this happened in the last 30 years? Well, maybe the first person didn't get started and disciple anyone. Or the third or ninth person didn't follow though and do their part. If everybody doesn't stay faithful and disciple one person per year, the model breaks down and the results are minimal in comparison. Looks to me like that is what has been happening for many, many decades.

"Discipleship, following Christ and embracing His mission, is the proof that our faith is authentic."

What will it take to change those results? I'm not sure. But I know this: If I do my small part and can convince my disciple to do his part, and more people would see the huge benefits available if they do their own small part, we might just have a chance to have incredible impact.

Phil Manginelli, founder and pastor of The Square, a new church plant in Atlanta, Georgia, commented in the CBMC Living Proof Adventure Series, "You can't just view this task (discipleship) as something you're into and out of as quickly as possible. It has to be a sense of a mindset shift. And now suddenly I have a mission field and this group of people that matter to me. And so, therefore, I have to create this margin or this space where I actually get to know them, get to hear them, get to understand them, and get to invest in them."

Again, Jim Peterson of The Navigators said, "So, what does a person need to continue to grow once he's come to Christ. Well, he needs some friends who will walk on the same journey with him, and he needs the Scriptures, and he needs the Holy Spirit."

Can you be that friend to walk through life with that person?

Of course, it's all in God's hands. But don't you think this is exactly what He wants to see happen? After all, that's the command Christ gave us just before He left: "***As You Go***, make disciples of all nations."

Greg Ogden of the Global Discipleship Initiative writes, "Believing without discipleship isn't really believing; it's just verbal or intellectual agreement. Real faith is a faith that follows, that obeys Christ's commands. Discipleship, following Christ and embracing His mission, is the proof that our faith is authentic."

We're not waiting on God to move; He's waiting on us to be obedient. So, join me and let's get going to impact at least one person for Christ, ***As We Go***.

Living It Out, *As You Go*

Key Points to Remember

- God loves you more than you can imagine, and God has a plan and purpose for your life.
- Isaiah 60:22 says, "One shall become a thousand", the power of spiritual multiplication and reproduction.
- Discipleship is the proof that our faith is authentic.

What Will I Do?

55. Do I have any real, authentic, caring relationships like the one Victor has with Brett?

___

___

___

56. If not, how could I go about developing a relationship like that?

___

___

___

57. Have I ever been strongly prompted to call someone and discovered the prompting was from the Holy Spirit? Has anyone called or contacted me when I was in serious need?

___

___

___

Final Thoughts

As you think back about the stories and what it looks like to share your faith, ***As You Go***, there are several common threads that you can find in many of the chapters and my experiences.

Here are the highlights:

1. Pray intentionally every day for God to engage you with the right people, ones that He wants you to impact and those that He wants to have impact you.
2. Be alert and expecting to have divine appointments.
3. Be willing to engage with someone to see what God has in mind.
4. Keep praying and stay in touch.
5. Be prepared and willing to share stories about what God has done in your life.
6. You do the sharing; God does the saving. Relax and have fun talking about Jesus.

It's not any more complicated or difficult than that. **We just need to do it!** Please join me and a multitude of ***As You Go Ambassadors*** in following the Great Commission command of Jesus to "make disciples," ***As You Go***.

Notes & References

PART 1

1. Scripture reference, Matthew 28:19, the New International Version (NIV), copyright © 1973, 1978, 1984, 2011 by Biblica.
2. Quote from Carl F.H. Henry, an American evangelical Christian theologian.
3. Craig Smith, Senior Pastor at Mission Hills Church in Highlands Ranch, CO.
4. Quote from Jimmy Carter, former President of the United States.
5. Quote from Theodore Roosevelt, former President of the United States.

Chapter 1

6. Scripture reference, Matthew 6:17, the New International Version (NIV), copyright © 1973, 1978, 1984, 2011 by Biblica.
7. Quote from Rick Riordan, *New York Times* Bestselling Author
8. Quote from Harry S. Truman, former President of the United States
9. The Barna Group, visionary research and resource company located in Ventura, CA, started in 1984.
10. Pew Research Center, a nonpartisan fact tank that informs the public about the issues, attitudes, and trends shaping the world.
11. PRRI– Public Religion Research Institute, American nonprofit, nonpartisan research and education organization.
12. *Outreach Magazine*, sharing stories of outreach, helping Christian leadership discover the ideas, innovations and resources that will equip them to advance the kingdom of God through the outreach efforts of the local church.
13. Quote from British theologian Smith Wigglesworth in 1923
14. Quote from Chad Hovind, Christian author, commented in CBMC's Living Proof Adventure Series, © 2019 CBMC, Inc. All Rights Reserved.

Chapter 2

15. Scripture reference, Ecclesiastes 3:7, the New International Version (NIV), copyright © 1973, 1978, 1984, 2011 by Biblica.
16. Scripture reference, Matthew 28:18-20, commonly referred to as "The Great Commission."

Chapter 3

17. Scripture reference, 2 Corinthians 5:20, the New International Version (NIV), copyright © 1973, 1978, 1984, 2011 by Biblica.
18. Quote from G.K. Chesterton, English writer, poet and philosopher
19. Dr. Darryl Bock, Executive Director of Cultural Engagement for Center for Christian Leadership at Dallas Theological Seminary, in an interview with Guy Rodgers, President and CEO of Pinnacle Forum
20. Scripture reference, 2 Corinthians 5:20, the New International Version (NIV), copyright © 1973, 1978, 1984, 2011 by Biblica.
21. Scripture reference, Matthew 28:18, the New International Version (NIV), copyright © 1973, 1978, 1984, 2011 by Biblica.
22. Scripture reference, 1 Corinthians 2:16, the New International Version (NIV), copyright © 1973, 1978, 1984, 2011 by Biblica.
23. Scripture reference, Philippians 2:5-8, the New International Version (NIV), copyright © 1973, 1978, 1984, 2011 by Biblica.

Chapter 4

24. Scripture reference, Matthew 22:37-40, the New International Version (NIV), copyright © 1973, 1978, 1984, 2011 by Biblica.
25. Quote from J Hudson Taylor, missionary and founder of the China Inland Mission.
26. Del Tackett, the creator of The Truth Project and the movie Is *Genesis History?*
27. Scripture reference, Matthew 22:36, the New International Version (NIV), copyright © 1973, 1978, 1984, 2011 by Biblica.
28. Scripture reference, Matthew 5:44 and in Luke 6:27, the New

International Version (NIV), copyright © 1973, 1978, 1984, 2011 by Biblica.

29. Scripture reference, Jeremiah 29:11, the New International Version (NIV), copyright © 1973, 1978, 1984, 2011 by Biblica.
30. Scripture reference, Matthew 22:37-40, Galatians 5:14, Romans 13:9, the New International Version (NIV), copyright © 1973, 1978, 1984, 2011 by Biblica.
31. Quote from Bob Goff in his New York Times Bestselling book, *Everybody Always.*
32. Quote from Jim Petersen of the Navigators.

Chapter 5

33. Scripture reference, Philemon 1:6, the New International Version (NIV), copyright © 1973, 1978, 1984, 2011 by Biblica.
34. Quote from Nelson Mandela, former President of South Africa and anti-apartheid revolutionary leader.
35. Phil Manginelli, founder and pastor of The Square, Atlanta, Georgia, commented in the CBMC Living Proof Adventure Series, © 2019 CBMC, Inc. All Rights Reserved.
36. Fabien Bouchard of Christian Refuge, YouTube, Big But, Church Media, Christian Sermon Illustration, Published 2/3/12.

PART 2

37. Scripture reference, Matthew 6:13, the New International Version (NIV), copyright © 1973, 1978, 1984, 2011 by Biblica.
38. Scripture reference, Ephesians 3:10, the New International Version (NIV), copyright © 1973, 1978, 1984, 2011 by Biblica.
39. Quote from Chuck Blakeman, author and founder of the Crankset Group
40. Scripture reference, Isaiah 6:8, the New International Version (NIV), copyright © 1973, 1978, 1984, 2011 by Biblica.

Chapter 6

41. Scripture reference, 1 Thessalonians 5:16-18, the New International Version (NIV), copyright © 1973, 1978, 1984, 2011 by Biblica.
42. Quote from C.S. Lewis, British writer and theologian – *The Chronicles of Narnia and Mere Christianity.*
43. Quote from Chad Hovind, Christian author, speaking in the CBMC Living Proof Adventure Series, © 2019 CBMC, Inc. All Rights Reserved.
44. Scripture reference, John 15:7-8, John 15:11-12, the New International Version (NIV), copyright © 1973, 1978, 1984, 2011 by Biblica.

Chapter 7

45. Scripture reference, Matthew 5:16, the New International Version (NIV), copyright © 1973, 1978, 1984, 2011 by Biblica.
46. Quote from St. Francis of Assisi, an Italian Catholic monk in the 12th century.
47. Quote from Martin Luther King, Preacher and Civil Rights Leader in the 1960s.

Chapter 8

48. Scripture reference, Romans 12:2, the New International Version (NIV), copyright © 1973, 1978, 1984, 2011 by Biblica.
49. Quote from Rick Warren, Founder & Sr. Pastor of Saddleback Church in CA
50. Ten Attributes of an Effective Marketplace Ambassador, © 2019 CBMC, Inc. All Rights Reserved.

Chapter 9

51. Scripture reference, Exodus 4:12, the New International Version (NIV), copyright © 1973, 1978, 1984, 2011 by Biblica.
52. Scripture reference, Mark 13:33, the New International Version (NIV), copyright © 1973, 1978, 1984, 2011 by Biblica.
53. Quote from Marc Ostrofsky, NYT Best Selling Author, Venture Capitalist, Entrepreneur.

Chapter 10

54. Scripture reference, Romans 12:11, the New International Version (NIV), copyright © 1973, 1978, 1984, 2011 by Biblica.
55. Quote from Oliver Wendell Holmes, Associate Justice of the Supreme Court of the United States.
56. Quote from Bob Goff, NYT Bestselling Author of *Love Does*.

Chapter 11

57. Scripture reference, Philippians 2:5, the New International Version (NIV), copyright © 1973, 1978, 1984, 2011 by Biblica.
58. Scripture reference, John 15:13, the New International Version (NIV), copyright © 1973, 1978, 1984, 2011 by Biblica.
59. Quote from Abraham Lincoln, former President of the United States
60. Quote from John Clear, Author, entrepreneur, and photographer.
61. "The Gospel Blimp", 1967 film adaptation of Christian author Joseph Bayly's popular satire.
62. Quote from Sean McDowell, CBMC Living Proof Adventure Series, © 2019 CBMC, Inc. All Rights Reserved.

Chapter 12

63. Scripture reference, 1 Peter 3:15, the New International Version (NIV), copyright © 1973, 1978, 1984, 2011 by Biblica.
64. Quote from J Kevin Earl, author.

Chapter 13

65. Scripture reference, Psalm 107:2-3, the New International Version (NIV), copyright © 1973, 1978, 1984, 2011 by Biblica.
66. Quote from Flannery O'Connor, American novelist and short story writer.

Chapter 14

67. Scripture reference, Matthew 22:14, the New International Version (NIV), copyright © 1973, 1978, 1984, 2011 by Biblica.
68. Quote from Brent M. Jones, Author of *Simply the Best*.

69. Quote from Del Tackett, Former president of Focus on the Family Institute, creator of The Truth Project and the film, *Is Genesis History?*

Chapter 15

70. Scripture reference, 2 Corinthians 6:2, the New International Version (NIV), copyright © 1973, 1978, 1984, 2011 by Biblica.
71. Quote from Germany Kent, American Journalist and Author.
72. *Daily Walk Bible*, Walk Thru the Bible Ministries, 1997, published by Tyndale House Publishers.

PART 3

73. Scripture reference, Isaiah 60:22, the New International Version (NIV), copyright © 1973, 1978, 1984, 2011 by Biblica.
74. Scripture reference, Luke 15:7, the New International Version (NIV), copyright © 1973, 1978, 1984, 2011 by Biblica.
75. Quote from Angie Karan, Australian blogger.
76. Kris Wilder's poem "My Friend" appeared in the March 16, 2011 issue of the Inter-County Leader, on page 41 A.

Chapter 16

77. Scripture reference, Galatians 6:9, the New International Version (NIV), copyright © 1973, 1978, 1984, 2011 by Biblica.
78. Quote from Kimberly Guilfoyle, American television news journalist.

Chapter 17

79. Scripture reference, John 9:5, the New International Version (NIV), copyright © 1973, 1978, 1984, 2011 by Biblica
80. Quote from Charles Spurgeon, English Baptist Preacher, "Prince of the Preachers"
81. Quote from Kirk Cameron, TV and Movie Actor, Christian Evangelist

82. Quote from Dave Rathkamp, Area Director of CBMC in Houston, describes *Lifestyle Evangelism.*
83. Spiritual Awareness Chart – Adapted from the "Engle Scale" by James Engle. What's Wrong with the Harvest. Grand Rapids, Michigan: Zondervan, 1975. Print (45)

Chapter 18

84. Scripture reference, Matthew 9:37-38, the New International Version (NIV), copyright © 1973, 1978, 1984, 2011 by Biblica.
85. Quote from Dietrich Bonhoeffer, German pastor and theologian, author of *The Cost of Discipleship.*
86. Quote from Billy Graham, Evangelist to the World.
87. Quote from Jim Petersen, in a video from the CBMC Living Proof Adventure Series, © 2019 CBMC, Inc. All Rights Reserved.
88. Definition of Discipleship from AllAboutFollowingJesus.org, © 2002-2018. All Rights Reserved.

Chapter 19

89. Scripture reference, 2 Timothy 2:2, the New International Version (NIV), copyright © 1973, 1978, 1984, 2011 by Biblica.
90. Quote from David Platte, Pastor of McLean Bible Church, NYT Bestselling Author.
91. Operation Timothy, © 2019 CBMC, Inc. All Rights Reserved.
92. Quote from Phil Manginelli, founder and pastor of The Square, a new church plant in Atlanta, Georgia, commented in the CBMC Living Proof Adventure Series, © 2019 CBMC, Inc. All Rights Reserved.
93. Quote from Greg Ogden of the Global Discipleship Initiative.

Additional Resources

Christian Business Men's Connection

CBMC (Christian Business Men's Connection) offers world-class programs, studies, and tools for Evangelism and Discipleship in electronic, paper, and video formats. Check them out:
https://advance.cbmc.com/as/

Marketplace Ambassador – Ten Attributes

This study will provide media rich interactive resources that equip individuals to live out the attributes of effective ambassadors for Christ in the marketplace.

Living Proof Adventure

This program is a small group video-based training series for lifestyle evangelism. In this series, you will see principles of "living proof" presented in compelling videos and real testimonies.

Operation Timothy

This effective program is a relational discipleship experience based on the Apostle Paul's great love and affection for Timothy. This extraordinary process is rooted in the Great Commission, "as you go, make disciples of all nations."

Leadership Coach Training

With Christian Coaching skills, we can develop a new wave of businessmen to represent Jesus Christ in businesses and cities, wherever the Lord takes them. This training can revolutionize the way you communicate and interact with people at work, at home, and anywhere you go.

AsYouGo Website

To make it easier for you to live out the Great Commission, ***As You Go***, and to help you "spark a conversation that impacts eternity", we will be offering t-shirts, caps, coffee mugs, journals and other items with a unique design and message, plus the ***As You Go*** logo.

The website also has helpful hints, useful instructions, and more personal stories to help you become a more effective Ambassador for Christ.

Special Offer – An inspiring song with the message of ***As You*** Go has been written in collaboration with Brian Davis. For a limited time, when you purchase a book or any item, you can download this song for free by going to www.asyougoapparel.com.

As You Go 2.0

My second book will be underway as soon as I finish publishing this first book. My plan is to write more stories about the experiences God gives me, ***As I Go***.

My hope and prayer is that you will ask God to help you get engaged and "in the game". And that you will soon have some interesting and amazing stories of your own to share.

I would love to read your stories and possibly share some of them in this second book. Please write to me at victor@asyougobook.com or give me a call on my cell at 303-918-5481. I'd love to hear your thoughts and questions.